Neither Left nor Right

Neither Left nor Right

Selected Columns

Tibor R. Machan

HOOVER INSTITUTION PRESS
Stanford University   Stanford, California

www.hoover.org

Hoover Institution Press Publication No. 522

First printing, 2004
10 09 08 07 06 05 04   9 8 7 6 5 4 3 2 1

Manufactured in the United States of America
The paper used in this publication meets the minimum requirements
of American National Standard for Information Sciences — Permanence
of Paper for Printed Library Materials, ANSI Z39.48-1992. ⊗

Library of Congress Cataloging-in-Publication Data
Machan, Tibor R.
   Neither left nor right : selected columns / by Tibor R. Machan
      p.   cm. — (Hoover Institution Press publication ; no. 522)
   Includes bibliographical references and index.
   ISBN 0-8179-3982-2 (alk. paper)
   1. Political ethics—United States.   2. United States—Politics and
government—1989–   I. Title.   II. Hoover Institution Press publication ;
522.
JA79.M323 2004
973.929—dc22   2003020260

Contents

AFTERWORD: LAST REFLECTIONS

Acknowledgments

Over the years I have written columns for many publications (and more recently for websites), including the *Wall Street Journal*, the *New York Times*, the *Los Angeles Times*, the *Chicago Tribune*, the *Chicago Times*, *Asia Times*, the *Cleveland Plain Dealer*, the *Houston Chronicle*, *USA Today*, the *Washington Star*, the *Washington Times*, the *Journal of Commerce*, the *Boston Globe*, the *Santa Barbara News-Press*, the *Goleta (California) Advisor*, *Laissez-Faire City Times*, *Laissez-Faire Electronic Times*, *Navigator*, *Ideas on Liberty*, and, on a regular basis since November 1966, the *Orange County* (earlier the *Santa Ana*) *(California) Register*.

This book contains mostly work I have prepared for Freedom News Wire, the distributor of my columns to newspapers owned by Freedom Communications. These columns have been published at different times by different Freedom Communications newspapers, although some columns aren't placed or dated. Many of them I was able to locate and date, but some were published without my knowledge. Of these, a few — marked with an asterisk — may never have been published but could have been picked up when they became available on Freedom News Wire at the "Columnist" folder on First Class, the electronic communications system of Freedom Communications. Some columns were retrievable, as well, from "Tibor's Forum," another folder on First Class, and could be used by Freedom newspapers by copying them from this folder.

I wish to thank Freedom Communications for permission to use the columns I've written for "Tibor's Forum," for Freedom News Wire, as well as for any newspapers owned by the company. I also wish to thank the other publications from which I have received permission to use my work in this book. And I wish to thank all the publishers for having given me the opportunity to air my views in their magazines, newspapers, journals, and again in this book.

Thanks also go to John Raisian and the Hoover Institution at Stanford University for the support I have received in collecting these short opinion pieces for this volume, and to Freedom Communications—especially Dick Wallace—for the financial help that made publication possible. David M. Brown was enormously helpful with editorial work, and the staff of the Hoover Institution Press has been very helpful in coming up with a final manuscript.

Preface

Since before I went to college, I have been writing columns for different publications. First it was just one or two for the paper at Andrews Air Force Base, then for my student newspaper, the *Associate*, at Claremont Men's College, and finally, beginning in 1966, I started to write for the *Santa Ana Register*. I have written for that publication since then hundreds of columns, becoming a regular columnist for the *Orange County Register* in 2001.

During these years I have also written for *Reason* magazine, which I helped found, the *Freeman*, *Liberty*, and other small magazines, as well as several columns for the *New York Times*, the *Los Angeles Times*, the *Boston Globe*, the *Houston Chronicle*, the *Chicago Times*, and a few pieces each for the *Washington Times* and the *Wall Street Journal*. Many of my columns have appeared on websites and have been translated into Spanish, Italian, and even Lithuanian. My book, *Liberty & Culture, Essays on the Idea of a Free Society* (Buffalo: Prometheus Books, 1989), contains many of my earlier writings. The present work reprints only a few of those, among them probably my first or second column for the *Register*, "Freedom: Local and National."

When I was a graduate student in philosophy at the University of California, Santa Barbara, one of the visiting professors from the United Kingdom, Ilham Dilman, scolded me for writing columns—who was I, at my relatively young age, to sound off on various issues; I should wait until I knew a thing or two more. The late Eric Vogelin, a prominent conservative philosopher, also told me, when he had me over to dinner at his Stanford University home back in 1976, that I should not waste my time with such trivia.

I am not sure I can answer these reproofs with some superior retort other than to say that I have believed it prudent and sensible to assert myself, at least, thoughtfully. For someone who escaped not only from a tyrannical country but also from the home of a brutal parent, the liberty to speak out on issues I care about is precious. I believe these missives have encouraged a reflective thought or two by many readers—and they continue to do so, judging by the volume of mail and email messages I receive from around the globe.

I am grateful to have had the chance to sound off on matters I believe important, especially on the threats to individual liberty in the United States and around the rest of the world. There may be interest in seeing some of the pieces I have written—and no more than perhaps one-fifth of my columns are published in this volume—put between book covers and made easy to have in one's library. Not everyone should speak on all important topics, and I have focused mainly on issues bearing on a free and just society—not on physical fitness, psychological self-help, or healthful eating habits, for example. Viva the division of labor!

To those who have encouraged me over the years I wish to give special thanks; to critics I also wish to express gratitude, since they have kept me hopping mentally, which is nearly always good exercise.

1. Foundations

Why Liberty Is Necessary for Morality

Yuma (Arizona) Sun, March 22, 2003

It is often taken to be a feature of a free society that it rests on the belief that no one can tell what is morally right or wrong. That is supposed to be why government doesn't impose a lot of strictures that people are forced to follow. If, however, we could determine what is right and wrong, then, the idea follows, government could just proceed to force everyone to behave right.

A sad result of so explaining the merits of a free society is that it begins to look as if liberty is the enemy of morality. And it is in just this way that a good many people have understood the Western tradition of liberalism. They have come to believe that if you accept the Western idea of a free society, you must not care about morality at all. Arguably, a great many enemies of the West hold such a view. Love the West, reject morality; love morality, reject the West.

Yet this is completely wrong. In fact precisely the opposite is true. The reason the Western idea of a free society makes a great deal of sense is that unless people make their own moral choices and act on them freely, there cannot be anything morally praiseworthy in what they do.

A person who does the right thing because it is commanded, forced upon him, isn't acting morally. Such a person is acting from fear, not from the conviction that what he is doing is right. It is only in substantially free societies that men and women can be morally good. If one is forced to praise Allah or God, give to the poor, or defend one's country, there is nothing praiseworthy about that. One is then a mere puppet, not a morally responsible agent.

Of course, there have been some who have defended the individual's right to liberty on the ground that no one can tell what is right or wrong. Some very famous people have done this. Yet their defense of human liberty is a weak, ineffectual one. That's because if one cannot tell what is right or wrong, one cannot tell whether violating someone's right to liberty is right or wrong. So a moral skeptic simply has no consistent reason to complain if the right to liberty is violated.

Those, however, who insist that they do know right from wrong have no justification for opposing a free society. For men and women to be morally praiseworthy—or alternatively, blameworthy—for something they do, they have to do it freely, of their own initiative, not because they are coerced to do it.

No one is morally improved by being forced to be generous, just, kind, courageous, prudent, honest, charitable, moderate, humble, or the like. The paternalistic motivation behind many government measures that ostensibly aim to make people good is hopelessly misguided.

I would even question the motivation of those who promote coercive government measures aimed at reducing vice and increasing virtue—since coercion kills personal responsibility and does this very obviously, it is more likely that advocates of forcing people to be good are power seekers, not promoters of morality at all. They use morality merely as an excuse to rule other people. In the name of an allegedly good intention, they perpetrate the most dehumanizing act; they rob people of their liberty to choose.

Of course, the laws of a free society cannot guarantee

that citizens will choose the right way to act. That choice is in the hands of the citizens themselves and their fellow citizens, friends, community leaders, teachers, writers, and others who urge us all to do what's right, not law officers whose task is keeping the peace, not making people good! But in a free society, where no one is authorized to dump the results of his or her misdeeds on others' lives, people are encouraged to do the right thing more than in societies where personal responsibility is missing because of a lack of individual liberty. So the critics of a free society who want more emphasis on morality than on liberty would do better if they first stood up to defend liberty. In a free society the prospects for a genuine, freely chosen morality are far greater than they are wherever men and women aren't free.

Is Human Nature Good or Evil?*

As a little Catholic boy, I was taught that we are all born in sin—we inherited it from Adam and Eve who defied God in the Garden of Eden. That is the story of original sin, and in most Christian religions one gets over it by being baptized. The theologians of Christianity, as well as the philosophers on whose thought some Christian ideas were built—Plato, Plotinus, and others—cooked up this idea.

Is it right? Are we really all basically rotten?

The secular version of this story is a bit different, but not that different: we all have some rather low instincts or drives that make us vicious, nasty, greedy, and only when we are properly socialized do we manage to get straightened out. This nonreligious version of the idea gained prominence through the writings of such figures as Thomas Hobbes in the seventeenth century, and Sigmund Freud in the nineteenth and twentieth.

Again, the real question is, are these folks right? Are we all tainted from the start—is human nature basically corrupt?

An alternative view has also emerged, both from religious and from secular sources. For the religious, it holds that the doctrine of original sin doesn't mean we are all base or lowly, only that we are capable of going bad, of getting corrupted. Young ones aren't evil, but they can become so, as well as good—it is a matter of our God-given free will.

Saint Augustine and Thomas Aquinas taught roughly this idea, as did Aristotle in ancient Greece.

For the secularists, it is a similar story: we are born innocent enough, by no means inclined toward good or evil, but as we grow up, our choices guide us toward one or the other, more or less. It is up to us; we aren't hardwired either way.

Of course, there is yet another idea, pushed by many natural and social scientists, that all this stuff about good and evil is nonsense—we just are what we are, as wolves, birds, whales, or ants are, and all the talk about good and evil is superstition or myth. But this view has its problems since those who hold it pretty much denounce those who don't, thus implying that the moralists are not doing right in holding their crazy ideas.

It looks, therefore, as if we cannot just toss out the notion that human beings can go right or wrong and do so on their own initiative. The only real question is whether they are predisposed to do one or the other or are free to do either.

But wait, isn't this just a question of opinion? Can these matters be settled? Haven't we tried fruitlessly to resolve them, all through human history?

One promising way to look at it is that yes, we have tried and have maybe even succeeded in finding some pretty good answers, but one generation's answers will not hold up automatically for the next. It seems to be a stable part of human nature to want to find things out for oneself, not just be told what others have come to think about basic issues.

So these basic questions, even if they have been dealt with successfully in the past, will recur again and again. Those who are dedicated to tackling them will continue to have jobs, one might say. It isn't like the sciences or technology, where we are always building on the latest advances, never mind what people did in the past. It's more like getting a job—just because mom and dad did doesn't mean I don't need to get one myself.

Now don't worry, I am not going to try to give some facile answers to all this—I would need volumes to treat the issues, if I were up to that in the first place. But I do wish to suggest something that may be of use.

When it comes to whether people are good or bad, originally or of their own making, it does not help any to inject government into the picture. Morality cannot be forced on people; it has to be something people choose on their own. A habitual, reckless gambler isn't going to be a better person if forbidden to gamble, nor will a greedy person become generous if others take his money and give it away. They may change because they become scared of gambling or of losing money but not because they have seen the light.

Another point is even more important. This is that if there is any impetus to wrongdoing, nothing works better to that end than placing extraordinary powers in some people's hands. We know this from common sense: the temptation to become a bad cop is considerable because the means to do it are greater when one is legally entitled to use a gun on other people. Power corrupts, as Lord Acton said, and absolute power corrupts absolutely.

Governments that have too much power become despotic, mainly because they cannot resist using the force at their disposal for misguided purposes—censorship, regimentation, oppression, privileging some at the expense of others, and so forth. The kind of power governments have works well only when properly restricted to certain retaliatory purposes.

So admitting that, for whatever reason, there is going to be bad behavior wherever we find human beings should not encourage us to think that this requires empowering certain folks—the government—to try to mend everyone's ways. Once these folks get the power to attempt to do that, they become the most susceptible to evil.

Evil in most cases can only be fought with social, not political, pressure, with education, with the influence of intimates and neighbors. It is useless to try to do it by making some people rule others—that only makes things worse.

What Free Will Is
and Why It Matters

Orange County Register (California), January 4, 1998

Free will isn't usually a topic for pundits, but I happen to work also in the discipline of philosophy, so I may be excused for thinking free will important and wishing others did, too. After all, it is vital to how we see human nature and conduct, ethics, law, and even international affairs.

The idea of free will is in deep trouble nowadays. First, this is what it means: we, human beings, have a basic and unique ability to be the primary cause of what we do. We are individually responsible for our conduct, unless we have sustained some serious damage in our brains. But normally, for those able to navigate their lives more or less successfully, free will is a reality.

Second, free will implies that since we cause much of what we do, we can be held responsible for the good and bad outcomes of our behavior. Our system of criminal law still sticks to this, more or less, though attorneys more and more resort to claims that their clients couldn't control themselves, had no free will. The famous defense attorney Clarence Darrow used to argue upfront against free will. Today it is an underlying theme in the defense of most who are accused of crimes — most recently, Theodore Kaczinski, who will probably give as his defense against the charge that he committed the crimes of the Unabomber that he lacked free will. But that defense still leaves open the possibility that others do not lack free will.

In the fields of psychology, sociology, economics, evolutionary biology — and even linguistics — there seems to be a consensus that free will need not even be mentioned when we consider how people think and act. All that we hear is that most of our behavior is caused by our genetic makeup or, alternatively, by our environment. Scientific reports on such debates have made the papers recently, and no attention at all has been paid in them to the possibility that we ourselves produce our behavior, as we choose, not as either our genes or our environment forces us to.

Most of the consensus about free will stems from the belief, embraced about four hundred years ago, that the world operates like a kind of clock. God wound it up, and since then it is pretty much running a predetermined course. Isaac Newton seems to have thought this — certainly many of his students supported the idea. Many philosophers, such as Thomas Hobbes, David Hume, Adam Smith, John Stuart Mill, Karl Marx, and others accepted the position, in some version.

The belief of these philosophers has left us with the view that nature makes no room for freedom. Only religion does, but there it becomes a matter of faith, not something that can be demonstrated.

Well, this view is misguided because nature does not really look the way early scientists thought it did — populated by tiny bits of matter colliding with one another in an infinite daisy chain. Nature is more complicated, made up of varied things, with diverse natures and abilities, so that human beings could very well have the capability, unmatched elsewhere, of causing their own actions. Some rare scientists have actually argued this — the late Roger W. Sperry, the Nobel laureate from the California Institute of Technology, did.

It is also pretty evident that we have free will if we just consider that nothing in nature makes us do the things we do; nor are we hardwired to do them, since many of us do not. Take writing poetry, composing music, devising multibillion-dollar mergers, or writing newspaper columns — or, indeed, almost everything human beings do — to do these things we have to take the initiative. Even to argue against free will or not to consider it is a matter of choice.

For purposes of our brief consideration of the topic, just think that when someone criticizes the free-will position, this means we ought not to hold it, does it not? Well, but that implies we have a choice whether to believe this or that viewpoint, and that pretty much assumes we do have free will. Otherwise why debate the issue?

Perhaps it is worth noting that although so many of the people concerned with how human beings behave give a cold shoulder to the topic of free will, in nearly every waking moment of our lives we assume that free will exists. This is clear from how much we criticize folks: such criticism — of people in politics, education, athletics, entertainment, business, law, science, and even philosophy (say, for misguided thinking about this very topic) — would all be beside the point if people couldn't have acted differently from how they actually did. It would all be "que sera, sera," and the critics would be uttering total nonsense.

Are they? All the time?

What Is the Nature
of Self-Interest?*

November 7, 1997

*The beauty of free-market capitalism is that it does not require
anything more than ruthless self-interest from its most ruthless,
self-interested citizens. When the system works properly, they
enrich us all by enriching themselves without giving the matter a
great deal of thought. If that is no longer true, it is not a sign that
people are less moral but that the invisible link between private
gain and the public good has been severed.*
 Michael Lewis, "Lend the Money and Run,"
 New Republic, December 7, 1992

Lewis's observation, made in an essay reviewing books by
Nicholas von Hoffman (*Capitalist Fools: Tales of American
Business, from Carnegie to Forbes to the Milken Gang* [Double-
day, 1992]), and James Grant (*Money of the Mind: Borrowing
and Lending in America from the Civil War to Michael Milken*
[Farrar, Straus and Giroux, 1992]), has several questionable
assumptions embedded in it. And they are all worthy of
scrutiny. For although some economists who champion the
free market embrace some version of Lewis's idea, their use
of it does not quite fit his characterization.

 First, Lewis assumes that we all understand what "self-
interest" means. But from the time of Plato there has been
serious debate about whether self-interest means "doing
what one wants" or "doing what one actually benefits from
(by some objective standard of what benefits a person)" or,
again, "doing whatever one is doing."

There is nothing remotely "ruthless" about doing the second, while the first is tautological, redundant. It amounts to saying no more than that people act because they want to act, so invoking it as a characterization of what they do makes little sense unless those who invoke it smuggle in some objective standard of what benefits oneself. The last way of understanding self-interest is what most technical economists mean: when we see people doing things, they are pursuing their self-interest. In other words, the self-interest referred to in economic analysis is really what Milton Friedman said it was in his Nobel prize acceptance address: "The private interest is whatever it is that drives an individual" (Milton Friedman, "The Line We Dare Not Cross," *Encounter* [November 1976] 11). By this account, both Michael Milken and Mother Teresa act from self-interest. In fact, however, this just means that both have their own motives from which they act. Their motives may be very different, and to understand their conduct it is this difference that is most significant. Knowing that they both want to do what they are doing and are, indeed, doing something isn't going to tell us a lot about the character of their acts. Yet that is all that being "self-interested" seems to mean here.

Second, Lewis's claim assumes that we know what it means for a system of political economy to work properly. But there is a great deal of dispute about that, too. Does a system work properly if it enhances justice? Or economic prosperity? Or equality of well-being? Or stability? Or peace? Or God's purposes for us as determined by reference to the Scripture, the Torah, or some other good book? Or all of these?

Indeed, those who talk along these lines may well have some hidden idea—hidden even from themselves—of what "work properly" means, usually, advancing some ideal they hope they share with their readers. But that hope is just what is mistaken, especially in this age of multiculturalism: there are too many competing social ideals, and by some accounts we aren't even supposed to ask which is better, which has greater validity.

Yet without addressing that issue, there simply is no way to determine what system of political economy works. For example, it needs to be shown that a system that achieves equality of opportunity or aggregate prosperity or protection of individual rights or spiritual enlightenment is better than a system that achieves some other objective. Yet when public discussion ensues concerning what kind of system works, it often seems that these matters are left untouched.

Third, Lewis's claim assumes that being moral consists of doing things not for oneself but for the public interest, understood in some way or other. We find in his remark a necessary schism between private gain and public good.

Just why are we to believe Lewis's assumption about what it is to be moral? After all, if the public is worth benefiting, why would not private citizens also be worth benefiting, even from their own actions?

Just because the public is large? But that assumes that mere numbers make something worthy. Yet a lot of scoundrels are worse than one good individual. Indeed, why should it be, even in simple altruism, that benefiting others is good but benefiting oneself is at best morally irrelevant? After all, the agent is also a person who has needs and wants, and why should serving those needs and wants rate lower than serving the needs and wants of others?

There are probably other assumptions involved here, but these are the ones of direct interest to us. The unabashed invocation of the Smithian doctrine, expressed so aptly by Bernard Mandeville in his *Fable of the Bees*, "private vice, public benefits," is instructive. It shows that we still embrace the conflict between the individual and the common good that gave rise to many of our troubles.

By this doctrine, people can exonerate themselves morally when doing something that is to their benefit only if this is done so that others also benefit. Moreover, even then one isn't gaining moral credit, only escaping moral blame. For if one does not benefit others while benefiting oneself, one's action lacks redeeming moral worth. The reason is that the agent is never taken to be worthy of benefiting from his or her actions, only others are. Yet, that makes very little sense—why should other people be worthy of concern but not the agent who acts?

Not only does this view condemn many people in business as lacking in all moral worth—those who are not guilty of moral wrongdoing but who have not made any positive moral achievement through their business successes—but nearly all artists, scientists, educators, athletes, and so forth, who do what they do because they judge it to be to their benefit, something they themselves value or find fulfilling.

Most great artists and athletes do not set out to serve other people but work because they have a vision they want to realize. The greatest scientists do not usually do their work because they want to benefit humanity but because they are intrigued by some problem.

The same view of morality that condemns people in business to moral irrelevance also condemns nearly everyone who isn't a martyr or a saint, which is already enough to call this view into question. This is one reason that when people in business try to defend what they do—namely, strive to prosper—they often pretend that it is for the public interest they do it.

So instead of such a sloppy approach to a vital problem, what needs to be discussed is just what kind of political economic system human beings should establish and maintain. If selfishness is understood as striving to make a good life for oneself, there is nothing to be apologized for. But if selfishness means something else, we really do not yet know what we are talking about since the term is being used ambiguously.

A final note: Just remember that when self-interested conduct is condemned, it indicts what we are, our self or ego. And if that is justified, if we are really no good, then there is no hope because even everything we do for others is done by someone who is morally suspect.

Freedom:
Local and National

Orange County (California) Register, December 10, 1966

So many of us have one of the fatal political diseases prevalent in our society that it would be of benefit to discuss this disease in detail.

I am speaking of the tendency in most of us to assert a particular political principle in one situation and at one time, while proceeding to deny it in another situation at another time. Conservatives, liberals, Republicans, and Democrats, almost all of us, have given ample evidence of this tendency. Few of us, however, realize that such tendencies, unchecked and unchanged, may lead to the downfall of all rational principles in our society.

The most blatant example of invoking a political and moral principle while denying it in the same breath occurred in 1964 when two propositions appeared on the California ballot, each one dealing with the problems of property rights. Proposition 14 concerned itself with the right of a homeowner to sell his home, directly or indirectly (through a realtor), to someone he chose on any basis he believed relevant. Proposition 14 thereby meant to reinstate the moral principle of the right to property on a legal basis. While it was known by many honest supporters of the proposition that many people voted for it or supported it because of their dislike for African Americans on purely irrational, that is, racist, grounds, they realized that since the principle itself was a valid one, it deserved their continued support

even in the face of having to accept the undesirable fellowship of racists. At any rate, most political advertisement for
Proposition 14 was based on the principle of property rights.

There was, at that time, another issue on the ballot that
concerned the principle of property rights, even though it
did not directly affect homeowners or raise issues of racism.
Proposition 15, which asked the voters to refuse the right
of subscription television to enter the marketplace, was also
on the 1964 ballot. This proposition was not similar in content to Proposition 14, but the principle by which one would
have supported or opposed it was the same. While Proposition 14 asked the voters to affirm a citizen's legal right to
act freely in the marketplace, Proposition 15 asked just the
opposite. It asked the voters to deny a corporation's legal
right (i.e., the right of a voluntarily combined group of people) to act freely in the same marketplace. Both propositions
concerned property rights, that is, the right of a citizen or
group of citizens (corporation) to use or dispose of property
as the owner sees fit, so long as no one is harmed through
that act.

As we all know, the voters approved both propositions,
though they asked for the establishment of diametrically
opposite measures. From this it should be clear that many
of those who voted had no idea concerning the principles
that were involved in their choice. Some may have simply
chosen to ignore them. Thus, distressingly, one may conclude that many of those who voted for Proposition 14 did
so without regard to property rights—having ignored or
avoided the question of property rights as they came to a
decision concerning Proposition 15.

Now, it is disturbing enough to realize that fundamental
moral and legal questions, such as whether a man has a right
to his property and whether one may enter the "free" market

as a businessman, are decided through majority rule; one would have thought that fundamental principles (basic rights, such as the right to life, liberty, and property) constitute the foundation of a legal system and are not open to the democratic process (just as the right to one's life is not periodically decided by majority rule). But not only is this not true at this time in our legal history, the fact is that the same group of people at once affirmed and rejected the very same fundamental legal principle within the context of the democratic process. Considering that the notion of the right to property ownership (property rights) is fundamental to the legal, economic, and political history of the United States, the fact that at this time its affirmation and denial happened with such candor and in such magnitude is that much more appalling.

Of course, these are but two instances in which people — which means, of course, a number of individuals — have acted or voted without regard for moral or political principles. Some other instances include those when people have opposed or supported zoning laws, blue laws, local ordinances which restrict some people from doing what harms no one at all (except that some consider it a "menace to the community"), and so forth. More frequent and far more intensive is the support of some people for the censorship of movies, magazines, and books that they believe are a "menace to the community." In every one of these instances, the people who support zoning laws, censorship, blue laws, and so forth, are affirming the rule of the majority over the minority. If, then, some of those who are violent supporters of such dictatorial measures have the audacity to cry out against "big government" or "centralized governmental power" when it comes to state or national issues, they are clearly rejecting the very principles they have supported. Accordingly, they have themselves among others to blame for the realization of such governmental power and size since they, in their ardent support of majority rule, have legitimized the principle of majority rule in all areas of public and private life—be it zoning, blue laws, censorship, eminent domain, public works, prayer in public schools, public accommodation, provisions under the guise of "civil rights," or whatever is put up for political decision.

The practice of complaining about the very thing that one has brought about or supported is so widespread that it transcends most ideological and political boundary lines. Republicans complain about government spending in the national government while they brag about it in state government, as if the two did not both spend the taxpayers' money; conservatives decry the power of Washington while they would love to gain power themselves and enact the laws that would bring about the "moral reform" of society; liberals complain about discrimination against African Americans while they themselves have for years discriminated against all of their ideological opponents in not giving them a hearing and in dismissing them as extremists; the left wing opposes the draft because it forces people to fight a battle they do not want to fight while the same left wing supports every government decision that contributes to the "Robin Hoodism" of distributing any person's wealth to those who did not produce it, that is, by forcing some to do something they might not want to do; the right wing supports the free enterprise system of economics with "the less, the better" government, only to turn around and ask for the prohibition of certain political groups' right to freely say or publish what they want, and so forth.

In the face of all the disturbing evidence of irrationality among this nation's political participants, what sort of lesson should one draw? Well, perhaps not all of us can learn from fact and from the evidence of the past. Some—and perhaps most—are not disturbed by the fact that in the area of freedom of action, be it intellectual or economic, this nation is on the downhill path and has been for several decades. That the country has not suffered uniformly from all this is due, mainly, to the initial momentum of this nation's economic success and technological achievement. Just as a very healthy man will not experience immediate disaster from having contracted a serious virus, so the United States has been successful in withstanding, in the main, the continuous attacks that it has suffered from within, attacks affecting its most vital properties, such as its legal system, which was designed to secure economic and political freedom for all citizens. The question is, how long can it keep on in this way, and how might we ensure that the health of the patient will take a turn for the better?

The most important thing that a person can do to achieve this purpose is to act in accord with the most fundamental principle of a free society. This principle is that no one may initiate force for any purpose whatever. If one were to follow this principle consistently, one would never vote for a measure that aims to suppress free action; one would never write to urge one's representative to vote for giveaway programs; one would act and urge others to act in whatever legal way possible to eliminate subsidies (which use taxpayers' money to support members of industries), to eliminate tariffs (which protect some business people against other, and often better, business people who offer better and less expensive goods), to eliminate public projects (which use some peoples' money to build parks, roads, industries, etc.,

and maintain forests, beaches, etc., for others), and to eliminate all foreign aid (which distributes the taxpayers' money
abroad to support goals considered wise by some people in
Washington and elsewhere).

Principles and
Flexibility

Orange County (California) Register, June 3, 2003

In contemporary American and, indeed, world politics, it is often considered a good thing to be flexible. Principled politics is dismissed by many as "ideology." Rather than ideology, we all ought to embrace pragmatism.

The term "ideology" has several senses. One is tied to Marx's claim that principled economic and political thinking is nothing but a rationalization for class interest. Those, for example, like Adam Smith and David Ricardo, who proposed a substantially laissez-faire, free-market system as being best suited to a community's economic organization, were supposedly doing this merely to promote the interest of capitalist, wealthy people who were well served by such a system. So, Marx believed, the principles of laissez-faire were a facade for class interest and were not held up on the grounds of their soundness at all.

Another meaning of "ideology" is simplistic political philosophy. In this sense, ideology provides knee-jerk responses, not genuine solutions, to complex problems. That is what critics of principled thinking suggest about people whose ideas they do not like, not that these people honestly develop and use political principles in an effort to understand what ought or ought not to be done by public officials.

Of course, people embrace different ideologies, and their own is usually construed as the result of long and hard thinking and observation of community life, issuing in judgments and evaluations based on such thought and observation. Others, with different ideologies, are, in contrast, thoughtless propagandists for simple, rigid, and unworkable answers and lack the flexibility that would produce realistic solutions.

Politics, in fact, requires both principled thinking and proper flexibility in the way principles are applied. Just as in law, there is a need in political thinking for basic ideas that serve as the foundation for understanding how human communities ought to function. But in law, it is also vital that cases that arise be considered in the light of the facts, many of which may be new and might even need modification of the principles that guide legal decision making. Is it in fact possible to develop principles about such matters as long-term public policy, or can we only handle problems case by case? Indeed, our Supreme Court, interestingly enough, prefers the second approach, seeing the first as involving dogmatism and rigidity.

Actually, principled thinking is indispensable. Just think of it—when one learns to drive, one needs to learn the principles of, say, defensive driving so that one can be ready to cope with the challenges of the road. Scientists strive to identify principles, in physics, chemistry, biology, and economics, and do not leave it all to learning piecemeal, bit by bit. Doctors are trained in the principles of medicine and good health and do not just look at a case as if it were brand new. And in ethics and politics, too, what we learn from history and human nature are principles.

It is pretty unrealistic to think, however, that only flexibility, case-by-case assessment, or that only rigid dogmatism, the unthinking application of various ideals, has a role in guiding personal conduct or public policy formulation.

Today the principled approach is largely avoided by prominent intellectuals because of the strong influence of America's homegrown philosophical school, pragmatism. Yet the attitude of these intellectuals is unrealistic, as my earlier points make clear enough.

What needs to be noted, however, is that there are those people in public life who find it useful to construe every problem as unique, thus leading to public policies and legal decisions that need not be adjusted to serve basic principles. This makes the people who administer law and public policy the ultimate arbiters of how things should go. This, in other words, defeats the ideal of the rule of law, an ideal that makes sense when the alternative is the rule of arbitrary human will, be it that of the majority, the king, or a single ruling party.

The ideal of the rule of law allows everyone to be in on the assessment of legal and public policy decision making — we can all check out whether our lawmakers and policy-makers are doing the right thing. If, however, no principles are available, then anything goes, and usually the most emotionally appealing choice is accepted, leaving those who express these emotions most effectively the purveyors of demagoguery.

Consider that in some areas even those who prefer flexibility draw back from this approach when it comes to certain issues. No one would think that when a man forces a woman to have sex with him, the act should be considered on a case-by-case basis, rather than declared as in principle criminal, or rape. The principle behind this classification is that a person has the right to choose with whom he or she will have sex. To dismiss such a principled approach implies a case-by-case approach, making it likely that unprincipled decisions, resting on the emotional appeal of perpetrators or victims, would rule. It is easy to imagine how juries, told to be flexible and to avoid rigidity, would base their decision not on the principles mentioned above but on whether the perpetrator was otherwise a nice person, had appealing attributes, served the community vigilantly, promoted economic prosperity, or painted well. A flexible approach would leave such decision making unimpeachable. But a principled approach, while still requiring attention to the details of the particular case, would ensure that in the end it was a violation of basic human rights to rape someone.

Is this mere ideology? Is it simplistic? Is it lacking in flexibility and pragmatism? No. Nor would it be mere ideology, simplistic, and lacking in flexibility and pragmatism, to judge various, say, political or economic matters by reference to certain tried and true principles, ones we have learned over the many years of human experience in community life.

Thus, for example, when someone objects to government intrusion in the market place, thinking it a violation of our economic freedom, this is not merely ideology but the application of arguably well-developed and established principled thinking to an understanding of public economic policy. Criticizing restraint of trade because, well, it amounts to interference with people, a violation of their private property rights and freedom of contract, is no less based on tried and true principles, not as they apply to one's sovereignty over one's sexual life but to one's sovereignty over one's property and liberty.

I would urge all the realists, pragmatists, and champions of infinite flexibility to consider that if they applied their view to all of what we do, there would be no basis for condemning lying, cheating, fraud, rape, murder, assault, kidnapping, or the other ways people damage their fellows. In politics, no less than in ethics or morality, there are some general principles that must come into play as we evaluate how people conduct themselves. It is a matter not of whether we need principles but which principles we in fact need.

The Proper View of Government

Navigator. Poughkeepsie (New York), December 1, 1998

As free-market champions make increased headway in the political and cultural arena, conservatives and neoconservatives have been taking more and more potshots at them. William Kristol and David Brooks of the *Weekly Standard* have been especially keen on denigrating the libertarian idea of a government with properly circumscribed powers and scope. Among the many charges lodged against that idea, the following seem most common: (1) Limited government is not inspiring. (2) Libertarianism provides no basis for patriotism. (3) Libertarianism provides no basis for a national leader.

Inspiring Government

The first allegation states that limited government is not sufficiently inspiring to rally the support of its citizens. Conservatives say that a government looked on with suspicion — thought of as a necessary evil — has little chance of surviving, let alone flourishing. Even the ordinary operations of government, they observe, require a modicum of respect from citizens. And in times of crisis, government must command devotion as well as respect.

Now, let it be admitted that, in the heat of debate, libertarians sometimes say things that do not bear close scrutiny. Thus, libertarians have at times made the claim that government is a necessary evil, and, in fact, that theme occurs in the writings of the American founders. But others in the libertarian tradition have advocated a strictly limited government without any suggestion that government, properly understood, is an "evil." John Locke, for example, assigned government an honorable role, even while insisting that none of its powers should violate basic individual rights.

Libertarians, then, can have a positive idea of the state, though their attitude to it will always be a demanding one. As the Declaration of Independence declares, it is to secure the rights to life, liberty, and the pursuit of happiness that governments are instituted among men, deriving their just powers from the consent of the governed. And what are those just powers? Only the powers needed to secure the rights in question—no more, no less. The task of the state is akin to that of a police officer: to apply the force needed to protect citizens, while avoiding unnecessary force. It is a tall order and a delicate one. And those governments that succeed in fulfilling the task are entitled to respect and devotion.

Consider the moral virtues such a government must have: vigilance, valor, honor, and most of all, integrity. These are values people greatly admire when embodied in soldiers, police officers, and judges. Suppose legislators and administrators embodied such virtues as well. Would they not earn the respect of the people, as statesmen once did? Certainly, they would earn more respect than they do by seeking power at all cost, legislating without regard for principles and the Constitution, meddling in all our concerns, and paying off contributors and constituents with subsidies and privileges. If those who love liberty are today uninspired by government, it is not because their view of government is too limited but because existing government has become degenerate.

Libertarian Patriotism

Recently, conservatives and neoconservatives have come up with another taunt against libertarians: what basis does their philosophy offer for patriotism? Again, libertarians have sometimes provided the Right with ammunition.

Consider the following incident. In 1987, Kris Kristofferson starred in a very bad miniseries called *Amerika*, which concerned a Russian takeover of the United States. Four years later, when speaking at the Republican Leadership Program Retreat, Cato president Ed Crane cited the miniseries in some amusing and profound remarks.

> At one point Kristofferson steps out of character and is about to say something intelligent. He's attempting to arouse the dispirited masses (not to mention the television audience), and he says, "America is not the land. America is not the flag. America is. . . ." And suddenly he has my attention, America is what, Kris? Here's what he says: "America is not the land. America is not the flag. America is the people. . . ." What Kristofferson should have said is that America is not the land; America is not the flag; America is an idea. And the idea is a fairly simple one. It's the idea of human liberty.

Now, that sounds good—until one realizes that ideas have no homeland. Walter Berns, the conservative constitutional scholar, has come at the same point another way, in an article entitled "On Patriotism" (*Public Interest*, Spring 1997): "There is, of course, nothing peculiarly American about those [the Declaration's] principles. On the contrary, they are abstract and universal principles of political right, a product of political theory; any people might subscribe to

them, and Jefferson himself expected that, in the course of
time, every other people would do so. 'All eyes are open, or
opening, to the rights of man,' he said on the eve of the
Declaration's fiftieth anniversary. This has not happened,
but were it to happen, America would lose its distinctive-
ness, and, along with it, any claim on the affections of its
people."

Surely, that is not true. Surely, it is too abstract. For it
is not just the principles of liberty that inspire American
patriotism but the ways in which those principles have
shaped the country's history and culture, including the attitudes of, yes, the American people.

For instance, in dealing with others, most Americans
have a certain casual confidence, a relaxed manner of social
intercourse, and an uncomplicated individualism. And
Americans like that about their countrymen. In that sense,
there is after all something to the remark that "the people"
inspire our love of country.

Of course, libertarianism has not yet been put into practice in enough places to offer us a true database of cultural
anthropology. Yet a bit of imagination would suggest that
love of country within a libertarian framework amounts to
a combination of reverence for certain basic principles of
freedom and an attachment to a set of shared beliefs, attitudes, and practices that either further those principles or
(at the least) are compatible with them.

National Leadership*

The last trendy charge of conservatives, a charge usually
associated with "TR Republicans," is that libertarianism has
no conception of a national leader, as opposed to a top
executive-branch functionary. Of course, if Theodore Roo-

sevelt is their model, one can only say, "Thank God libertarianism excludes such a leader." A free country has no need for a leader who sets about running the country according to his own idea of the good life. Quite the contrary, a free nation's leader should remind citizens how noble it is to set one's own goals. Perhaps that is why generals have typically made bad presidents.

Still, a country does need a leader, at base because it needs someone to serve as the final guarantor of national security (although other symbolic roles accrue to such a leader). Were America suddenly attacked by nuclear missiles, the president would and should have it within his prerogative to launch a retaliatory strike, even if that brought utter destruction to the United States. It would and should be within his prerogative, despite Congress's power to declare war and despite the Supreme Court's power to declare presidential acts unconstitutional. The president alone is and should be vested with the ultimate power to act, when necessary, on behalf of the nation. Locke, in particular, spends much ink on spelling out how such a prerogative is part and parcel of the executive branch of government, even though the government must be held accountable once the emergency has passed in which the prerogative was exercised.

As a result of this fundamental leadership role, the president also takes on the role of serving as the symbol of our national values and as the voice of our national sentiments.

It is true that in libertarian political philosophy, because of how much emphasis is placed on simply showing that there is merit to its basic principles, these special areas of concern have yet to be fully developed. Still, if the American experience is a reliable clue, there should be no great difficulty in envisioning a robust sense of patriotism and loyalty, as well as a basic respect for, even devotion to, a libertarian administration. Few people in political history have inspired as much diligent study and respect as the founders of the American republic, especially on the part of those who have experienced the devastating effect of tyranny. An idea of government that stands as history's greatest bulwark against such tyranny is anything but dispirited. Conservatives in America, of all places, should not be tempted to think so.

The Merits of the Slippery Slope*

May 26, 2002

In the study of arguments, the slippery slope has a dubious reputation. If, for example, one argues that, after government acquires the legal power to censor, say, sex and violence on television, it can in time begin to acquire the authority to censor even political ideas, this is often scoffed at as alarmism, nothing really worth worrying about. Why? After all, the logic isn't bad. When government gains legitimate power over the content of movies, books, or magazines, why should it matter what the content is? Any content is threatened, even if at some particular time only some of it is actually targeted.

Well, for one, the slippery slope argument isn't about what is likely to happen, only about what can happen. In America, for example, the tradition of freedom of speech is pretty strong for political speech and weak for commercial speech; so even though by the logic of the law it is possible to extend censorship to what people write on politics—this is speech, after all—it isn't likely to occur, at least not just yet. But, should people start losing their attachment to this tradition of political free speech, the law may no longer stand in the way, protecting us against censorship. And that is because the slippery slope is, in fact, a motive force of public policy.

The law, for example, attests to this in how precedence works: if certain areas of human conduct have come to be subject to government regulation, similar ones can also become subject to it. Most recently, for example, after the tobacco companies were made subject to lawsuits and government regulation because they supposedly caused people to become addicted to smoking, a good many state prosecutors began experimenting with lawsuits against gun manufacturers and even food producers. There have been efforts afoot, in Connecticut for example, to use the same strategy against food manufacturers on the grounds that they supposedly cause people to become obese and should be held responsible for this.

But, and this is where slippery slope arguments lack full conviction, although something in them may well be logically compelling, people are not always willing to follow the logic. They will not allow some matters to be swallowed up by what is called the logic of the law or public policy, simply because people do not want to go that far.

In America, for example, government has the power to regulate commercial speech—at least the courts, including the Supreme Court, have been ambivalent and have often permitted legislatures and regulators to limit advertising and other commercial speech. Of course, strictly speaking, if government may do this, there is no principled reason that it may not regulate other forms of expression, such as what is put on the wide screen or even in publications. For a while the Securities and Exchange Commission (SEC) even wanted the power to regulate the content of financial newsletters, never mind that this was a clear case of regulating written expression, something most of us figure is protected from regulation by the First Amendment of the Constitution. But once exceptions are made, the zealots will take it as far as they can—they believe they are good enough and wise enough to regiment our lives, so once a foothold has been gained, they certainly will not hesitate to exploit it if they can. The same trend is now in the works for the Internet. Only cultural tradition, expressed in some measure of public opinion, stands in the way.

Often, for example, there is an unabashed, unapologetic call for censoring movies for their violent or sexual content, and politicians, sensing that the public often feels appalled by this kind of content, are willing to test the waters. Some courts have resisted, but others haven't — in some local communities censorship has been rampant and, without a sustained legal challenge, has remained in force. Now, a good many Americans share the puritanical sensibilities behind this effort at censorship, which is why there has been considerable success on that front for the censors, even if it hasn't reached national proportions. (In France, which many intellectuals believe is such an open society when it comes to sexual mores, many sexually explicit movies are banned outright, mainly because the French have no constitutional protection akin to the First Amendment. And European Union courts have also censored books critical of, well, the bureaucracy in Brussels that guides this union!)

But there is a lot besides sex and violence that is quite offensive in movies. What about really off-the-wall ideas, paraded before audiences, day in and out, both on the wide screen and on television? Some shows promote lying, adultery, laziness, or sexism, no holds barred. And sure, this could quite possibly influence many who are watching. Other films promote the idea of how it is OK to ruin one's life if one's parents have brutalized one as a child. Many similarly dangerous ideas are treated as perfectly acceptable in movies, plays, and novels, not to mention popular music. Or consider movies that even quite recently treated communism as, well, just a misguided ideal, not a vile system

such as Nazism. NPR regularly features Soviet recordings
of famous music but would never do this with similar Third
Reich recordings. HBO's recent movie on Churchill gave
excuses for Stalin while condemning Hitler in no uncertain
terms. Offensive and dangerous ideas are rampant in many
highly praised films, as well—Woody Allen's *Crimes and
Misdemeanors* pretty much suggests that murder is no big
deal if you don't get caught!

In a free society men and women are officially taken to
be trustworthy, mature enough to deal with dangerous
ideas, be these about sex, violence, or political ideology.
Once that belief is given up, even for some extreme cases,
the slippery slope process can start. It may not always be
followed through, because different traditions and social
practices may slow it down or even stop it. But the law and
public policy will have been corrupted in the process.

At that point, all that is needed for the further erosion
of individual liberty and other principles is for a large part
of the population to get all riled up about something,
enough to match the force of tradition, so the slide to tyranny will not be far off. It is thus important to heed the
slippery slope and not worry about those who debunk this
argument as alarmist. Those who are wary of the slippery
slope are, instead, prudent and responsible.

The Right to Post One's Sign

Yuma (Arizona) Sun, December 28, 2002

The basis of nearly all freedom is the right to private property. If I am to be free to publish, I must be free to own printing presses and such; otherwise, my freedom has no meaning—if the government owns the presses, it has the power to revoke my liberty by simply denying me permission to use them. Just ask the journalists who worked for *Pravda* in the old USSR!

Indeed, whenever you own something, you are supposed to be free to do with it anything peaceful you might want. And by "peaceful" is meant whatever doesn't violate anyone's right to do as he or she sees fit in his or her sphere of authority, a sphere identified by one's right to private property.

Several years ago, in a canyon across from my home in Orange County, California, the owners of a pretty big plot of land built three white crosses. The crosses have been standing there above the canyon in the plain sight of all, be they Christians, Jews, atheists, or agnostics. No one to my knowledge has made any fuss, although some may find it annoying to have to look at a religious symbol they do not honor in their own worldview.

Why no fuss? Well, because we all seem to realize that when you have come to own something—either through your hard work or because you inherited it—it is up to you how you make use of it. It's an extension of your indisputable ownership of your self. Indeed, this is the basis of self-government, of the idea that in a free society the consent of the governed is required in order to have legitimate authority to govern!

Sadly, these days such reasoning has lost nearly all of its appeal in our "free" country. For example, in a recent court ruling about a citizen's right to place a sign on top of a surf shop in San Clemente, California, the issue wasn't settled on the basis of whether the citizens had ownership of the shop. That wasn't in dispute.

Instead the issue was whether the city authorities in San Clemente had banned the display of signs clearly and unambiguously enough. The judge declared that since the city's ban was vague, the surf shop owner was permitted to display his ten-foot wooden cross for the time being.

The implication is that if the city authorities had only drafted their ordinance more precisely, it would have been fine for them to prohibit the display of the cross on top of the shop. Yet one of the main reasons we want to own things is that we supposedly can then do with them as we choose, not as others choose.

Those folks across from my home who own the land there ought not to be told whether they may or may not place three white crosses on their property—they have a right to do so and should need no permission from a bunch of politicians or bureaucrats or even neighbors. Indeed, who are such folks to dictate to their fellows, as if they were little children, what they are allowed to display on their property? This to me is most puzzling. "Just who do you think you are?" should be the question these folks are asked. Indeed, they should ask themselves that question.

It was Abraham Lincoln who said, "No man is good enough to govern another man, without that other's consent" (*Collected Works*). That principle is the very foundation of a free society. But if one has no right to one's property, and a bunch of citizens can elect some blokes who then can tell others how their property may be used, then those others can legally be governed against their will, in defiance of their consent. And that is rank injustice.

In a free society people will, of course, have wishes about the composition of their neighborhood—whether, for example, advertising or religious signs are to mar the view. But in a free society the way such matters are decided isn't by imposing the will of some on the will of the rest, even if the former are the majority. That would simply mean a version of tyranny, that of the majority, which is hardly an improvement over the tyranny of some dictator or single political party.

No, in a free society one's wishes are supposed to gain support only voluntarily, through the consent of others. That means that if some do not want to see a sign placed on the property of another, they must use persuasion to get the sign removed, pay off the owner to get it removed, or, if none of that works, just turn their gaze away. They may not forcibly remove the thing, as if the property belonged to them, or send the police out to do the deed for them.

Alas, such principled thinking is not fashionable. Too many Americans have become unrestrained democrats who believe that simply being in the majority renders whatever they decide to do perfectly acceptable. That this belief would have justified slavery at one time, or the lynch mob, or the destruction of democracy itself (for example, in the Weimar Republic, which elected Hitler and imposed his dictatorship democratically on Germany) seems to escape those who cling to the myth that majority rule is sufficient to justify some policy. Indeed, if we generalized that idea, most Americans would become the slaves of majorities abroad!

The bulwark against the tyranny of the majority, no less than against one party or dictatorial rule, is the institution of a vigilantly protected system of private property rights. Sure, it may mean some cumbersome maneuvers in deciding issues in our communities. Yet, that's a small price to pay for the liberty it would secure for all citizens to live by their own judgment instead of being forced to kowtow to others when they do not want to.

Follow-up to the American Revolution: Abolish Taxation

Mises.org, April 13, 2000

The only good tax is no tax. Why? How would we fund government without taxes? These are good questions to ask. But first let's understand what taxes are.

Throughout most of history, governments—usually monarchies headed by kings, emperors, pharaohs, or other tyrants—actually owned everything under their rule, including, believe it or not, the people. In those regimes the people were regarded as subjects, not citizens. That means that people were treated as underlings, subject to the will of the ruler.

In these social systems, the institution of taxation was a cruel measure of outright subjugation, imposed by rulers on their subjects. Because the rulers owned everything, when the subjects lived on the rulers' land, the subjects had to pay for this privilege. No, they had no legal right to the land they worked; they had no legal right to their own labor; and none of their basic rights were given legal protection. The law affirmed the full power of the rulers, period, until gradually this absolute power began to be checked and contained.

In time the idea gained prominence that those who made up governments were human beings, not gods. Thus it dawned on many that they had no (divine) right to rule anyone at all other than themselves. The idea began to gain headway—between the eleventh and the eighteenth centuries—that every person had the basic, natural right to his or her life, liberty, and property. Anyone wanting to gain the benefit of another's work or other assets would have to ask for it. Sovereignty lay with individuals, not with governments—that is the central point about being a citizen as distinct from a subject.

This is the significance of the well-known phrase "consent of the governed." Consent must be obtained to govern a citizen, unlike a subject. And in a fully free society there are no exceptions. John Locke, the English political philosopher, went the farthest—though still not all the way—toward the development of this idea and its implications.

All the while, of course, the point had been resisted vehemently by those who felt they knew how others ought to live their lives (i.e., conduct themselves and make use of their property) and insisted that they could know it much better than the people on whom this "knowledge" was to be imposed. They fought tooth and nail, with force of arms, with references to tradition, and, of course, with fancy but mostly sophistic arguments. And the debate is still going on.

But not widely enough, and there is a reason for this. Like all extortion, taxation is difficult to fight. Moreover, in taxation the very people we call on to resist criminal extortion are the enthusiastic, loyal extortionists.

Judges, politicians, police officers, the agents of different branches of government—all those parts of the system that the founders of the American republic called on "to secure these rights"—have remained, as in feudal times, the very people who perpetrate the extortion: they have, as a matter of fact, become worse than extortionists, who, after all, know they are criminals. Those in government and their supporters who defend its supreme role in society often believe, sincerely, that their institution is a necessary, albeit coercive, agency, akin to a parent or guardian of children.

These folks are convinced that what they provide is so vital to us all that they do not have to ask for permission to provide it, so long as a sizable number of citizens—through some kind of democratic process (but one to which not all have consented)—back them up. No, they may impose their public services, never mind whether consent has been obtained from all those who are to be benefited and from whom payment, or taxes, are confiscated.

If the American founders had all along been preached to by the intellectuals who enthusiastically defend the institution of taxation, well, there would be no United States of America, the bastion of individual liberty in the world, and no glimmer of the hope of extending its ideas to further regions of human life. That is because from the start the leaders of this country had the revolutionary gall to call for more liberty for its citizens than those in other countries had. This call has been seriously eclipsed by the call of our current leaders, who do not even see the point of mentioning, let alone expanding, the protection of individual liberty as one of government's central tasks.

Of course, calling for liberty didn't always suffice, which is why slavery had to be abolished, for example, and why there is so much more work to be done along the lines laid out in the Declaration of Independence. All in all, despite compromises and failures, the call for more individual liberty has been one of the cornerstones of America's uniqueness.

The call for abolishing taxation, heard only here and there, mostly in demands for tax cuts, is just a further step in the direction of living up to the promise of the American Revolution. Ultimately, taxes need to be replaced with a form of payment for government services that is fully, uncompromisingly consistent with the principle of "the consent of the governed." Barring such a development, all we have is the chance to press the point: reduce taxes, privatize services, and through these acts, make us all more free.

2. How to Think

The Fashionableness of Thinking "Out of the Box"*

This is one of those phrases that has been thrown about a lot during the last few years, a kind of trendy expression that seems to put those who use it on the side of the angels. Think "out of the box." Look at things "out of the box." Don't be some old fogy, get with the program.

Well, in my humble view most folks who give this advice have in mind that you should think out of your box by starting to think in their box. And that is a natural wish, only it would be nicer to get the straight dope on it, not have it dressed up as some kind of wise insight—as if the people urging us to think out of the box had such a nifty handle on how restrictive our box is and how open and inventive and exploratory it is outside of our (and inside their) box.

To be sure, human beings often get stuck in a certain mode of thinking, although this is not always a liability. Much of what we accept and live by nearly automatically, without much scrutiny, is tried and true and indispensable. Traditions, customs, even laws arise, often, because after much rumination and reflection over the years, decades, and centuries a good many of us have intelligently enough decided that these are worthy ways to approach the problems we face. So scoffing at these ways, the insides of our boxes, is arrogant—as if what's new and untried had some kind of natural claim on being sound and brilliant. More often, however, the novel approaches are purely speculative and manage to be impressive only because they are rather vaguely laid out and no one quite knows how to assess their merits. It isn't so simple to forge a revolution, actually.

I recall back in the late 1960s, when the student revolution was in full force, both here and abroad, a great many of the academic practices we were used to were derided as fuddy-duddy. One such practice was grading. It was not cool to grade students anymore. Why? Well, because it was simplistic, uninformative, rather staid and rigid. After all, what does getting an "A" or a "B" or a "C" mean, anyway? It is a ranking, but what is the reasoning behind it?

Well, for a while professors who just wanted at all cost to be on the side of their hip students caved in and abolished grades. Entire institutions were written up in *Time* and *Newsweek* for banishing that middle-class tool, grading, from their systems. In its place professors gave consultations and made comments that laid out explicitly just how students had done in their courses. No longer would we take shortcuts but talk it all out with every student in detail.

But it turned out that those new ways were, well, just the old ways refashioned. For what did an "A" mean? It meant and still means, to anyone who would just use his mind a little, that the student's grasp of a subject was superb and that he or she managed to state it clearly and cogently and knew better than the rest the different schools of thought about it. And so on down the line. It really was no great mystery what grades meant, and a little reflection made it clear that the point of using those letters was, well, economical. They were like arrows pointing at intersections — why write out the elaborate "To get there you need to go this way" when using an arrow was simpler and more economical and took much less space on a street sign.

Not that all innovations are pretentious. But putting the

chairs in a class room in a circle and having a professor sit with the students as if, well, he or she were not really a professor but just some guy hanging out, didn't amount to anything very inventive and novel, after all. These innovations were mostly devices by which people faked serious reform. They made it appear that something productive had been thought of and introduced, while in fact it was all mostly a ruse.

I happen to think that all the talk about thinking outside the box is little more than this kind of ruse. An innovation, to have genuine worth, needs to be carefully and repeatedly tested. It needs to be compared and contrasted, not simply made to sound cool. Of course, it can be intimidating to be told that you haven't caught on to the contemporary, to what is progressive and advanced. You are thinking inside the box, doing what is routine, old-fashioned, and unchallenging. OK, but show me. Prove it to me, do not just throw around a bunch of jargon and invent some hip phrases. Give me the whys and hows, and then, perhaps, I will abandon my old ways of thinking, which have, after all, managed to bring me quite a way so far. As one old but useful saying had it a while back, "Where's the beef?" If you can show it to me, then I might change my ways for you!

The Cult of Feeling: Reason versus Emotion

Orange County (California) Register, September 30, 2002

In recent years one of humanity's most important discoveries—not inventions!—has been receiving a lot of flak. I am talking about human reason. If it isn't some multiculturalist claiming that being reasonable is just a cultural bias of Western origin, which has no universal significance (and cannot be used to criticize people who do not choose reasonableness as their standard), then it is someone who wishes to indict us all for the arrogance of thinking that human beings by reasoning can know a thing or two and make this or that, as well, that amounts to an achievement. In the late 1960s and early 1970s, the Age of Aquarius was supposed to displace the age of science and reason, meaning we were supposed to give up our prejudice in favor of reasonableness and embrace our feelings uncritically, since the tool of criticism is reason, and that, of course, is just another bias.

Mind you, this is no new story. From the time human beings started to record their thoughts, those who were hostile to thinking quickly took up their pens and produced reams of text denouncing (often quite thoughtfully!) thought itself. This battle, maybe the secular equivalent to that between God and the Devil, will probably go on forever. Reason versus unreason, reason versus unchecked feeling, reason versus impulse, reason versus intuition—the terms may change a bit, but the idea is the same.

No, I shall not jump in to resolve the conflict. This is not the forum for such an ambitious undertaking, even for a little portion of it. But it is worthwhile to note something odd about the misanthropic distaste for reason and the preference for feeling or emotion in the context of the equally virulent dislike of many famous folks for the human ego. Selfishness, you see, is supposed to be a bad thing. Unselfishness is good, or so many tell us—except, of course, our shrinks, who get paid to help us fix ourselves, selfishly as all get out.

There is a kind of reckless self-indulgence or selfishness that is unseemly and needs to be discouraged. Human beings who lack generosity, a sense of community and fellowship, can be a nuisance and, indeed, lack a good deal in their lives, thus verging on a failure to be selfish in the proper sense of that term. (Such terms, by the way—terms like freedom and justice and democracy—are constantly debated, so no one definition is widely accepted for them.)

That reckless kind of selfishness, however, is just the sort that goes hand in hand with the cult of feeling. This is because when we are guided mainly by feelings, not by reason, we are left pretty much on our own. Who else's feelings can we know better than ours? We feel thirsty, hungry, angry, jealous, envious, annoyed, playful, or whatever, and that is the end of it—how can we be sure what others feel? That would take reasoning, learning by rationally analyzing our experiences, and here reliance on feelings just cannot help.

The advocacy, therefore, of living by the guidance of feeling alone is pretty much the most antisocial, crudely self-centered advice you can give people. If you have nothing but your feelings, you can ignore others, certainly anything that would do them any good, which would take diligent rational thought to find out. You just feel this or that way, and that is the end of the story. You then act on those feelings. Since feelings are self-centered, you live a self-centered life. And even "self-centered" does not tell enough of it—you actually live a mere feeling-centered life, leaving the rest of yourself out of it, neglected.

I am someone who holds that rational selfishness is healthy, and egoism of this kind is right for people to practice. But since I also think human beings are by nature rational animals, this selfishness requires us to be reasonable, to listen to reason, if you will. And reason is very likely to tell most of us not living in tyrannies that cooperation with others, caring for them, is a sensible thing. Cruelty, violence, disrespect for the rights of others, and lack of concern for the well-being of friends and family are extremely unreasonable, selfish things. But if feelings are to guide us, then the only way we can be is self-centered, self-indulgent in the crassest of ways.

So, I suggest we heed Socrates, who reportedly said: "Not for the first time, but always, I am the sort of person who is persuaded by nothing in me except the proposition which seems to me the best when I reason about it."

The World from One's Own Point of View[*]

Too many people believe that they have their own view of the world, as does everyone else, and that there is no way to see things as they really are. This used to be a respectable approach to values, but now it is applied to nearly everything, even science. Some feminists argue that throughout history males have imposed their own viewpoint, even on the natural sciences, so that we have gained a distorted understanding of reality. Others hold that there is an Asian or European or African outlook on things. Or that each person sees things his or her way, period. There is no right answer, only my answer.

Common sense clings to the idea that if we try hard enough, if we watch out, we can learn how things are for real, without distortion. We take it that a careful scientist or detective or jury will get to the truth of things. Maybe not final truth but truth nonetheless. This is the source of respect for scientific research and, also, the source of the moral lambasting of racial, ethnic, sexual, and other prejudices. To prejudge, to judge before we get the evidence, based on some rash generalizations from loosely examined similar cases, is irresponsible.

But with certain influential thinkers this commonsense idea has come under serious criticism. Mind you, it is difficult to see how this could even be considered criticism, since to criticize is to assume you have standards that apply

to all and are not idiosyncratic. But, never mind, even consistency is often denied its traditional role as a necessary
part of getting things right.

But, you may say, why worry? Isn't this all just so much
academic babble, the fare that separates those eggheads
from us sensible folks? Not really. In many ways the rest of
us have bought into this relativist, subjectivist trap.

Consider that in the Microsoft debate it is now generally
understood that no objective position is possible; it is all a
matter of where you are coming from. If you like Microsoft's
products and services, well, then you are against the recommended antitrust actions the Department of Justice
champions. If you are a Netscape or Sun fan, well, then you
want Microsoft to sink. Kind of like rooting for your favorite
sports team — who really is good at the game isn't something
we can even talk about, it's all partisan.

Consider that in politics it is all relative, too. Some people just like the American system of quasi-capitalism, others
do not. As the Elian Gonzales fiasco shows, it is all a matter
of point of view. Those in Little Havana cannot help wanting
Elian to remain here, probably to bolster their own political
biases, while those who like heavy-handed state meddling
in our lives find nothing wrong with sending a six-year-old
kid back to Communist Cuba. No right answer is really
possible; again it depends on where you are coming from.

Consider the matter of gay rights. If you are a homosex-
ual, hey, naturally you will want to have unions between
members of your group seen in the favorable light of ordinary marriages. If you are heterosexual, then, of course, you
won't. Partisanship is the norm, and objectivity, a myth.

Consider, finally, that if you are male, you will just look
on all criticism coming from feminists as male-bashing, and

if you are a female, you will see any complaints of feminist extremism as the first sign of male oppression.

Many more areas could be highlighted as exhibiting this contemporary view, that we just cannot help seeing things from a perspective we somehow inherited or have because of our race, gender, or background. In the end, though, none of that makes sense since the idea that we all have a point of view simply becomes just another point of view, without a chance to be right, true, justified, correct. No, it too is just some point of view and not worth a higher standing.

Sure, we can be influenced by many factors, unique or common to some of us, such as height, color, weight, ethnic background, family upbringing, and so on. But do these constrain our minds as a harness constrains a draft animal?

One thing is for sure. With this reckless emphasis on point of view, we are liberated from the responsibility of making sure we get things right—in law, in journalism, in scholarship, or even in scientific research. So we need not worry about making mistakes, being accurate, or even being fair—the value of these, after all, is just a matter of where you are coming from.

What Do You Mean, "We"?

Orange County (California) Register, October 14, 2002

As I was listening to KNX-AM, Los Angeles' CBS radio affiliate news station, a few days ago, the station manager, George Nicholas, was giving his editorial comments, something he has been doing for over thirty years if my memory serves me right. This time he was talking about people in need of shelter, and he said, among other things, "we shelter" such and such number of people in the city of Los Angeles.

When I heard this, my mind left the main points of his editorial, and I began thinking about what this word "we" means. Does it mean that Mr. Nicholas is among a number of volunteers who shelter some people who need it, at the volunteers' homes (or other places that they own)? No, I am nearly certain that's not it—you probably will not find homeless people at Mr. Nicholas's house now or anytime soon, although I am not in a position to know this for sure— it's just an educated guess!

Or perhaps what he meant is that all the citizens of Los Angeles are providing shelter for some people these days. Only, this isn't right either, since many citizens of Los Angeles have no interest in doing this, may even believe it is wrong to do so, because they prefer to take a "tough love" approach to dealing with at least many of the homeless. In any case, many Los Angelinos are not in favor of sheltering

the homeless or, at any rate, all of the homeless being shel-
tered at city expense in Los Angeles.

Well, then what must "we shelter" mean anyway? I am
pretty sure what Mr. Nicholas should have said is that "in
Los Angeles such and such number of people are given
shelter by city government officials, and this shelter is paid
for with taxes." Sure, it may take a bit longer to say. But so
what?—it would clearly be more accurate than suggesting
either that there is a group of volunteers, to which Mr. Nicholas belongs, who give shelter to the homeless or that everyone in Los Angeles has come together freely out of the
goodness of their hearts to shelter the homeless. Neither of
these suggestions is true, yet "we shelter" those who need
it must mean one or the other.

In fact the use of the word "we" in public affairs is mostly
a travesty. It serves to perpetrate gross inaccuracy, not
always through mere oversight but more often through
intentional deception or, at best, sloppy thinking.

Those who claim, for example, that "we owe it to such
and such" might like us all to have such an obligation, but
in fact, they offer nothing to back up what they are saying.
When some folks say, "We want zero tolerance of drug use
or gang violence," it is clear that they do not mean it literally
or precisely. Many, many people in fact do want plenty of
tolerance toward drug users or even toward violent gangs,
so the speakers simply discount them, implicitly declaring
them nonpersons, noncitizens.

The "we" in these and similar contexts functions, in fact,
as a grand ruse or ploy, akin to how "we" was used in the
days of monarchies when the king presumed to speak and
act for everyone—all his "subjects"—because of the myth
of the king as the divinely ordained "parent" figure, God's

stand-in here on Earth. Bad habits often take a very long time to overcome, and even in America, where the founding political act was to abolish a monarchy in favor of a republic, the myth continues to be accepted as reality that the government speaks for us all on all matters of significance. But this is, exactly, a myth and a repulsive and dangerous one at that.

There are very few matters people in free societies care about equally. We have vastly, and often justifiably, different goals, purposes, tasks, and worries. To pretend otherwise is an attempt to dupe us into thinking that those folks who use the royal "we" have somehow managed to make their own concerns those of every one of us.

But they haven't! We — and here the "we" is right — better realize that!

If we do not, then we will all find that at one time or another we are being conscripted into a group whose membership we never sought. But because we paid scant attention to, and even went along with, the ruse, we will be treated as unwilling members. All the rules, to which we didn't consent, all the dues we did not agree to pay, will be imposed on us whether we agree or not. Through this abuse of the term "we," the idea of the consent of the governed will be eviscerated.

Of course, these liars and cheats shouldn't need to be reminded that they have no moral authority to conscript others in this way. But then criminals should not rob and rape and steal, though they will anyway. And to deal with this we have to be alert, careful, prepared.

It was the idea of the American founders that government is instituted among us to secure our rights. Sadly, by now, government has become the most vigorous rights-violator in our midst. One important way to make an advance toward remedying this is to heed very carefully what politicians and their allies among us say and catch them at each turn when they engage in verbal deception.

Calculating Bad Side Effects

Yuma (Arizona) Sun, August 24, 2002

Enemies of SUVs and other suspected environmental hazards (such as boats and airplanes) are telling us that the
personal benefits of an SUV (or boat or airplane) ride must
all be compared to the terrible public side effects. Economists refer to these as "externalities"—a word coined to
make it appear that we can deal with these matters entirely
without reference to values. (Social science, being a science,
is supposed to be value-free, if you haven't heard this yet!)

Yet what is at issue is clearly very much a matter of values
or the lack of them. It is the practice of imposing burdens
on unwilling others while enjoying benefits oneself. Secondhand smoking is supposed to be such an externality,
which is why so many call for bans on smoking wherever
others may be imposed on when smokers light up.

In some instances, however, while it is imaginable
enough that certain practices both reap benefits and impose
burdens, it is difficult, if not impossible, to determine the
costs and the benefits or indeed the identity of those being
harmed and benefited. Take SUVs.

True enough, big, gas-guzzling cars, whether trucks,
SUVs, old station wagons, or what have you, produce more
pollution than small ones. This is a burden, at least on first
inspection. The added smog, for example, can cause problems for nearby inhabitants, such as eye irritation, respira-
tory ailments, and so forth. There is also the possible loss

of vegetation and animal life over the long haul, which is easily seen to be an ill effect of pollution.

Yet, gas-guzzlers also produce benefits—they are safer in certain respects than other vehicles, they enable people to haul their own stuff around (e.g., when they buy an arm chair or dresser, they don't need to pay for its delivery but can take it home themselves). SUVs, for one, are easier to get into or out of, which for some people—especially those with physical impediments—is a significant advantage over having to squeeze into a VW bug or something similarly economical and environmentally friendly when it comes to gasoline consumption. And yes, there is the SUV's ability to pull boats or horse-trailers or to climb up some dirt road into the mountains. There could well be many other benefits for all the different SUV owners, as well as some hazards no one has yet thought of.

Despite this list of the costs and benefits of SUVs, or similar vehicles, it is by no means easy to compare the two, to determine which on balance is greater or smaller. The attempt to do what is referred to as a "social cost-benefit analysis" on SUVs and similar pollution-producing devices used in public places is nearly futile if not outright impossible.

One reason is that roughly the same people who benefit from SUVs could also be hurt by them. Also, although often when people do what can benefit or harm them, they isolate themselves from others—so the costs and benefits are confined to themselves and do not spill over—with air pollution, especially, this is not possible. All the stuff that is being carried by trucks on our highways, shipped by airplanes and boats, all the services produced by those traveling in SUVs, small trucks, or minivans, may cost people less because the externalities or side effects are dumped into the public sphere and need not be taken care of by vendors. If every truck had to pay the full cost for transporting goods, including the cost for all the pollution damage it creates, the cost of transportation would be much greater than it is, even to the very people who are hurt by pollution. If the cost of pollution created by SUVs and such were completely absorbed by those who own the vehicles, the owners wouldn't be able to spend a good deal of their wealth on other things that produce employment throughout the economy. Or their wages would have to be higher, preventing others from receiving wage hikes. These and similar results are all very complicated, indeed probably impossible, to measure.

However, understanding what is going on need not be very complicated. We can bring it down to a personal level. Sometimes, for example, one has friends—or pets for that matter—who are both pleasant and irritating. One then decides whether to hang out with—or on to—them based on what is more important, the harm or the benefit. Say a good pal of yours smokes. So, the only way to be around him is to put up with secondhand smoke. But he is such a fine pal that it's worth it, so you put up with the smoke despite its danger to you. Yes, this is something you can usually control—you might, if you are very vulnerable to tobacco smoke, just give up the friendship.

But when it comes to pollution created on the road, including that created by SUVs, just how much benefit we all get as opposed to how much harm, is impossible to tell. *This is because the realm is public,* and all the people involved, with their highly diverse wants, needs, and wishes, cannot be separated from one another. There is no effective way to measure the trade-offs, only very rough, unreliable guesses.

This indeed is one reason why arguments about the

environment get so nasty. Those who want a pollution-free world want the power to shut down things like SUVs, no matter what; those who like their SUVs, on the other hand, don't want any restrictions placed on the use of their handy vehicles. There simply is no way for each side to leave the other to stew in its own juices.

Environmentalists cannot just move to some region completely cut off from SUV side effects (a move which may also be very costly to them, of course), nor can SUV owners merrily continue to use their vehicles and live with their own self-created pollution to their hearts' content. We are, as it were, in the same boat, and sorting out the costs and benefits, while it would be helpful, is quite impossible—a tragedy of the commons!

The reason a lot of us have been urging more and more privatization is just this: when practices are carried out on private property, they are more easily confined to those who carry them out. There are distinct borders. People can stay inside and keep their private property in a shape they prefer. Others can be kept outside if they will not accept one's terms of association.

This is not the case, however, where privatizing is impossible or at least very complicated. So, the issue then will often be fought out politically, a solution that hardly anyone finds satisfactory. Compromises are involved; the giving and taking of ground occurs where no one really wants either to give or to take.

OK, so what about it then? Well, for one, the beginning of wisdom here is to recognize that there is no higher or lower moral ground in these disputes. Environmentalists aren't saints for despising SUVs and the like, nor are SUV owners innocent victims who are being unjustly pestered about their own private business. Unless effectively privatized, the use of the roads (or the waterways or the air mass) will remain inherently controversial.

The goals of all those concerned on either side of the disputes may well be equally valid—good, so no one group can pretend to be on the side of the angels. The best bet is to recognize that neither side is going—or even deserves—to win a full victory for the time being, while we must carry on in the public realm and cannot cut ourselves off from others whose ways we dislike and who dislike ours.

3. The Independent Self

Why Moral Virtue
Is on the Wane

Yuma (Arizona) Sun, September 21, 2002

Talent, like wealth, is often important but mainly for its potential merit. There are talented people who waste their talent, who misjudge what it is good for, who mistake it for wisdom, and who get all enamored with themselves simply because, well, they have it. The same applies to folks with wealth. It's a bit like being taken with oneself just for being good-looking or tall or handsome. But it's what one makes of the talent one has that counts, and then how sensible one is about its scope or reach and how dependable one is in delivering on the potential one possesses. Similarly, when one inherits wealth, it's how one applies it that counts for merit, not having it.

When my daughter was about five, she and I wrote a little book together that we called "Cute Is Not Enough." It was a rather amateurish way to help her realize that just being good-looking—and it was clear to me then that she was and would be when she grew up—would not take her far enough in life. Another useful title could well have been "Talent Is Not Enough."

Both beauty and talent—and for some it could be inherited wealth—are assets with which people are endowed by birth. To make something of these, one must, as the old saying goes, apply oneself. And the rules of application, aside from the special skills required in any profession, include ethics, the skill for living properly, decently, or morally. In morality, the virtues are the skills everyone needs for living a good or excellent life, including courage, honesty, prudence, generosity, temperance, moderation, and so forth.

One might look at it this way: In life, as one reaches maturity, one takes an oath—just as one does, implicitly or explicitly, on entering a career—to do as well as one can. And as one goes about fulfilling this oath, one draws on one's assets, whatever they may be, to give one's life the best chance of successful development. But one also needs the benefit of general principles to follow, as one makes use of one's talents and other assets. By adhering to the universal, basic principles that ethics identifies for us, we keep on a reasonably steady path of development, whatever the details may be. Folks who fail to heed these general principles, who lack moral virtue, or character, in other words, may have many other assets but will most likely misuse them, abuse them, and carry off a kind of malpractice of living as they go on to their careers, in business, medicine, education, auto mechanics, the performing arts, or whatever. You can find such folks everywhere, including in the headlines—corrupt politicians, business professionals, medical quacks, and so forth, are all in this category.

Some people in different lines of work, including business corporations—no more nor less than people in other areas (politics, education, science, technology, the ministry, what have you)—just try to live off their potential, and those who trust them, unwisely, think that merely by giving free rein to this potential everything will be hunky-dory. And, of course, now and then, by accident rather than through character, determination, and commitment, one can cash in on sheer smarts, raw savvy, and other "talents." It just isn't a reliable way to go. Virtuosity is no substitute for virtue.

Yet, in our age, it is somewhat understandable that moral virtue is not the aspect of one's life and profession that most people focus on. Intellectuals—philosophers, educators, playwrights, authors, pundits, politicians, and the rest—have been teaching and preaching that what really counts is not being ethically rigid but being flexible, expedient, pragmatic, open-minded. Like the Constitution, the principles of ethics are considered out of date, organic or mortal, rather than steady and lasting. This is the message of postmodernism and its kin, deconstructionism and radical pragmatism. The belief in ethical principles is, for all too many intellectuals, something naïve and even uncouth. Embracing ethics firmly, consistently, is often dismissed as ideology or simplistic rigidity by many prominent, smart thinkers.

Of course, if moral virtue is discredited, perhaps only virtuosity is left as a common enough standard. For example, in academe, and especially in professional philosophy, where standards of right conduct are routinely challenged and viewed by many with skepticism if not outright cynicism, people are judged almost exclusively by how clever, quick-witted, smart, or "brilliant" they are.

So, when those educated at elite institutions, including business schools, fancy what makes them good, they are not encouraged to consider their character—decency, dependability, trustworthiness and the like—as their foremost asset. No, it's got to be something value-neutral, such as IQ or brilliance, and the self-esteem and self-confidence these assets engender in those who are so regarded. Virtue, in short, gets little respect from contemporary thinkers. They are skeptical of its very possibility.

Government and Business—
Some Telling Differences

Yuma (Arizona) Sun, August 31, 2002

Competition goes a long way to make those with whom we deal act polite, not ornery, and to make their establishments user-friendly.

As my daughter and I sat during a recent court appearance waiting to be called, with not a clue given about how long this was likely to take, I noticed that every sign in the building that spelled out some rule was put in terms of an order. "Shirts must be worn. "Smoking is prohibited." "No cell phones are allowed." And so on and so forth. Clearly, the tone of these notices conveyed to us all who was in charge, never mind that all those working there, from the police officers, judges, and legal aid attorneys to the security guards, were paid from money confiscated from us all at the point of a gun—by taxation, that is. The bulk of those who work for government do not even pretend to like the people for whom they work, especially not ones who are accused of having committed some infraction of a rule governments have laid down, be it major or minuscule.

In contrast, even when a private business tells us about some government regulation that we must obey, these notices are often put in terms of requests. "Your cooperation will be appreciated," even though it is a law! "Please buckle up," even if it is mandated by the federal government. This is even more true in restaurants, where smoking is prohibited by state law. There is usually a plea attached, if only as a matter of form.

This all suggests to me that most government (public) servants are latent petty tyrants from the word go — this attitude of issuing orders seems to be in their very bones. They do not even pretend to ask or suggest or propose or even implore, no. They know they've got the guns behind their myriad of rules, and they talk the talk of those with guns, not of those who perform a service.

Why is it that in the private sector even government-imposed rules are conveyed in a more polite fashion? Well, it is pretty simple.

We have a choice to deal with this or that airline, so the airlines treat us like royal subjects, even when the airlines are just messengers of the state. Sure, they have rules, and they may insist on our following such rules, quite apart from government mandates. Insurance companies often insist that private businesses adhere to rules and that their customers obey them — as when we are asked not to use the drive-up window as a walk-up window!

But, despite the mandatory nature of such rules, they are usually laid out for us politely. If you happen to light up in a bar or restaurant, at least in California, the proprietor does not eject you summarily but first asks you to desist. Not so if you do anything wrong at the Department of Motor Vehicles (DMV) or courthouse or similar public realms. "Keep off the grass," orders the sign in the public park!

All this brought to mind the time, in 1994, I visited Sofia, Bulgaria, and stayed at a government-run hotel left over from the socialist era. The surliness of the "help" was notorious. They were perturbed when customers came because, well, the help were doing the customers a thankless public service, not dealing with them in the ways of commerce where competition and the desire for return business put smiles on people's faces. Shortly after that trip I learned that in the Czech Republic a school had been started for people who dealt with the public in a market economy, to teach them that the surliness they were used to as socialist functionaries would not garner them many customers under even a quasi-capitalist system.

One bad habit of bloated government is that the officials seem to do everything to alienate people from the system. Just consider the prevailing—although not uniform—attitudes of those who deal with the public at the DMV. One might think, well, in courthouses and police stations most people are probably not very nice or have done something that may warrant a measure of surliness. But at the DMV?

Sports in America

Irvington-on-Hudson (New York) Freeman, September 1989

When I arrived in the United States from Hungary in 1956, one of my laments was that Americans didn't do as well as they could in the Olympic Games. The Soviet Union and other Soviet-bloc countries did comparatively better, as anyone who was familiar with the record could tell.

Everyone in my family had been involved in sports. My father rowed and later became one of Europe's better rowing coaches. He even coached in the United States for a while, at Philadelphia's renowned Vesper Boat Club. My mother was 1942 foils champion in Hungary and is still a coach in Salzburg, Austria. My stepfather was a saber fencer in Budapest and is today the U.S. Olympic fencing coach. My sisters were top swimmers in Budapest. I myself did a little of everything, until I decided that I had other priorities and confined myself to just exercise, not serious athletics.

One advantage of being an athlete in Communist Hungary was that if one showed talent and perseverance, one's life was made much better by the state. Under most statist political systems — ones that hold the state as a higher being than the individuals who compose it — sports become a public exhibition of collective excellence. That was especially true in Hungary and is still true in most of the Soviet-bloc countries, as well as in China and in some rightist states such as South Korea. If one demonstrates ability and willingness to become a world-class athlete, one is freed from all the normal responsibilities of life and is kept in considerable luxury and privilege. For this one sells one's soul and, especially, one's body to the state for as long as one's body holds up.

In my ignorance of the American political tradition, I was appalled at how little investment the American government made in amateur athletics. I noted that, with all its fabulous talent, America could win at virtually any of the Olympic events, if only sufficient resources and discipline were invested in that goal.

But of course here is the rub. American society may include some of the greatest talent for practically any task, including any aspect of athletics. But it is not primarily a statist system. Government in this society is—or at least is supposed to be—a servant of the people. Individuals and their own goals are of paramount importance, not showing off the system, proving to the world how fabulous the social organism happens to be.

Therefore, in America many of the Olympic events are truly amateur sports. Of course, there are exceptions and gray areas—tennis and basketball, for example. But in the main, the athletes compete because that is what they want to do. And these athletes often have a variety of goals in their lives, which shouldn't be surprising for relatively free men and women. Unlike, for example, the East German swimmers, many top American swimmers take time from their training to devote to studying, family, and fun. Why not? Life has much more to offer than being a single-minded athlete. Sport, after all, is supposed to be something of an enjoyment in one's life, not a mission of slave labor.

But I didn't understand this when I first came to the United States. I was a converted nationalist and didn't realize that what made this nation worthy of respect had little to do with winning the most medals at the Olympics, having the most productive economic system, being first in space, or any other single purpose that some people might want to take as a sign of collective success. What was vital for this nation was that each person had the liberty to strive for his or her own goals in life, as long as he or she didn't trample on the similar efforts of others.

So now when I watch the Olympics my thinking and emotional responses are different from when I first came to the United States. I scoff at the nationalism injected into the commentary. I am usually bemused and even elated, in contrast to the network commentators, when the Americans are not doing as well as the Soviet-bloc athletes — who usually appear glum even after delivering a 9.95 performance in gymnastics!

Free people do not put all their energy into a showy project such as the Olympics, except, now and then, spontaneously. Thus the 1984 Los Angeles Olympics disturbed me, although I realized that most people were celebrating the rejuvenation of the country, of which the American athletes' success in Los Angeles was something of a symbol. But some of the nationalism began to grate on me.

I am a refugee to the United States not because it manufacturers Olympic winners, or the greatest technology in the world, or any other single achievement found in it, but because it is the best environment for people to pursue happiness, according to their own individual talents, abilities, and choices.

Celebrating Liberty,
Not Conformity

Orange County (California) Register, April 28, 2003

America's culture and political system can be distinguished from the rest of the world's and from those of much of human history. There is, of course, a lot here that is no different from everywhere else, some great, some OK, and some pretty bad. But what America has more of than most other places is human liberty.

Sure, not all have it in sufficient abundance. Other countries actually have more in certain areas — for example, in much of Europe you are free to smoke and use drugs, and clubs are allowed to stay open late at night. All in all, however, there is much more freedom in America than elsewhere.

This is vital because freedom is a prerequisite of morality, of acting ethically — people aren't morally good when they are forced to behave well. However eager some may be to make us all good, it is simply an impossible task.

Also, freedom is necessary for individuality to flourish. In many societies and periods of history, the reigning idea is "one size fits all." Even the greatest thinkers have made this terrible mistake of thinking that one kind of life is best — even healthy — for everyone. It is from this that we got communism, fascism, totalitarianism, and other regimes where the objective has been or is to make everyone conform to one vision of human excellence. But no such vision can possibly work because we are unique in the living world in being essentially individuals. Yes, we are social beings, too, but this side of us does not violate our individuality if our human nature is respected, honored.

What I am saying here is actually not tough to prove. Just look around and notice how many decent people are quite different from one another. Some are adventurous, some not, some are loners, some are gregarious, some introverted, and some extroverted—the list could go on and on. Our goals, talents, tastes, and personalities are highly varied, yet oh so human. This is what individualism acknowledges—that we matter as individuals, not as parts of some greater whole. No one can be replaced as the individual he or she is, and we all know this at least implicitly.

Now in America this is more or less consistently understood. And the price we pay for it is that we realize that what others do, for better or for worse, is something over which they have the final say, however much it may displease the rest of us. The great cost of individualism is also its great benefit: an enormous variety of ways to live, both well and badly.

In America this idea is pretty much accepted, at least at gut level, even while many people bellyache about it endlessly. All sorts of pressure groups want to have everyone conform to their agendas, to their priorities, yet even as they want this, they accept individualism in many areas of their lives. Such are the contradictions of our culture.

Those of other cultures, however, are often more severe. In most places the individualist idea hasn't sunk in despite the evidence for it all around. The main source of all the diversity around the globe is just that people are individuals, apart from whatever else they may be. They have given rise to countless varieties of practices, traditions, philosophies, religions, styles of art, special sciences, and customs of food and dress.

What makes America irksome to many is that it was designed to accommodate a great deal of human variety; so it cannot in all honesty offer a utopian, one-size-fits-all vision of social life. With all this variety there is little hope of getting people to march to the same drummer, to follow the lead of just one guru — or even just one variety of fitness trainer.

And that cannot but annoy those around the globe who want to continue to rule people along such lines.

A Modest Look at Self-Importance

Orange County (California) Register, October 8, 2001

Jay Leno annoyed me his first time back on the air after the September 11 massacre when he said his own job was utterly trivial compared to what the police and fire fighters did in New York City, which lead so many of them to perish. I disagree and suspect he was trying to be profound but missed an important point.

No doubt, some folks are scared to take on risky work, but most of us know that risks go with life itself. Each time we get on the road, board a plane or train, even move around near our homes, we run risks. We also expose ourselves to criminals by simply living in the midst of civilization where they hide and prey on innocents to avoid having to fend for themselves through productive work. Doctors, dentists, accountants, comics, actors, directors—yes, even teachers and columnists—do what is necessary to pursue the work that suits them and gives them a living. We are all contributing, in a great variety of ways, to the flourishing of not just ourselves but of those who count on us to deliver something we can deliver and that they find of value. We are, one might say, all moderately important, only how this comes through is not always visible or dramatic.

Jay Leno, for example, as well as his colleague David Letterman and his predecessor, the highly successful host of the *Tonight Show*, Johnny Carson, may not contribute to our lives with dramatic works, but they amuse us, often just as we try to relax and close our hectic days. I cannot agree that this is anything trivial. It is no more trivial than is, say, Shakespeare, Rembrandt, or Chopin. There are differences between these and the stand-up comedians who entertain us nightly, but in certain respects they all address important aspects of our lives, more or less successfully. At any particular time, of course, one line of work can be far more significant than another, but this does not diminish what we all do, not at all. We still need to focus, carry it off competently, diligently, on time, considerately, and productively.

Why, then, are some people so tempted to demean what they do? I think the reason is that so many of those who lay out ideas for us—in novels, movies, opinion columns, and commencement speeches—promote humility, deride pride as if it were vanity, and want us all to submerge our egos in some collective mass where no one stands out.

Oddly enough, it is our individualism—the view that we have a right not only to life, liberty, and the pursuit of happiness but to living well, acting freely and creatively, and succeeding at happiness—that is so often derided by the commentators of our time. And, even more important, it is just that individualism and determination to live well that annoys so many people about us abroad.

But consider this: In most societies throughout human history the tribe is what came first, which meant that the tribal leaders' goals came first, and everyone else had to submit to the leaders' will. That means that individualism was a great threat to most societies, at least as the tribal leaders would have liked those societies to be.

Indeed, America is unique for having placed on record, in a very public way, the idea that you and I and our works matter and are not dispensable in deference to an elite that runs society—the kings, dukes, lords, sheiks, or commissars who would wish us to abdicate the task of living successfully so that their visions could be given full support.

Yes, America is different in its outlook on social life. It is not the tribe that is most important to most of us but our lives and the lives of those we have chosen to be with. And this is an irritant to tyrants across the globe. But it is nothing for us to be ashamed of. Indeed, it is why we attract so much quiet admiration and jealousy from the ordinary people in most societies and the main reason they want to be here with us rather than suffer an officially inferior status in their own societies.

How Would You Like
Being Unfairly Disliked?

Orange County (California) Register, October 22, 1992

For a while in my life, I suffered from the misconception that if I didn't like someone, it had to be because the person had some moral fault. This misconception seems to be a problem for a lot of people.

In the earliest stages of our lives, we get the notion that if we don't like Bobby, the next-door kid, or Susie, our kid sister, or, especially, Aunt Helen—it must be because these people have something wrong with them. But that is really too bad.

Someone should have straightened me out about this early on in my life—I might have gotten into fewer fracases, made fewer enemies, offended fewer folks, and remained on good terms with many more. Instead, I made the mistake of thinking that everything I didn't like in another person must be blameworthy. Not!

The fact is that we do not manage to develop a taste for everything possible to like, to be, to do. And those who have other tastes, other preferences and likes, may not strike us as pleasant.

I really do not like football. Nor baseball. Nor hockey. Nor going to the circus. Nor Roseanne. Nor Murphy Brown. No, I don't like a whole lot of things I encounter in life. I even dislike some of these things: very long skirts on women, Fords, Greyhound buses, and so on. I dislike country western music but love blues. And the list could go on.

But the point is, what does it matter? It only means that it would be best for me to stay away from what I dislike and near what I like and love. I need not—nor need anyone else—take that extra step of condemning what I dislike. So what if it does not please me?

Indeed, one aspect of individuality is that we have our peculiarities. I am a great fan of the color orange. But does it serve to indict others if they do not share this preference of mine? By no means. Their particular lives are such that they have developed different likes and dislikes, some of which may clash with mine. But clashes of likes and dislikes are a far cry from moral conflicts, even conflicts of aesthetic judgment. There is plenty of room for us all, with all our different rankings of what there is in the world around us to relate to, without having to pick on one another on the grounds of such differences.

When I accept that another person likes X, which I dislike, I am not making a moral compromise—I simply realize that this person is not the same as I am. And this understanding may be the clue to how we should appreciate members of different cultures and civilizations.

There is so much unnecessary strife in the world, often because people treat their preferences, tastes, or lifestyles as if these had some universal quality that everyone must honor or be damned for not honoring. Yet it is difficult to tell why some of these differences amount to anything morally significant. After all, we know that Hungarians like more spice in their soup than Danes do—and we do not consider that a ground for morally differentiating between them. Perhaps we ought to see the differences in other aspects of our lives in the same light—as simple differences, not as conflicts between good and evil.

Of course, there are the practices and traits of character

that we shouldn't simply dislike but should condemn as wrong, evil. But it can be a tough task to find out which these are and what we should do about them, if anything. At least we should give more thought to the difference between those aspects of other people's lives that we simply don't want much to do with, and those that we should regard as bad. With a better understanding of the difference, we might spare ourselves a lot of personal and, indeed, international strife.

4. Sex and Politics in America

The Crisis of Trust

Orange County (California) Register, September 16, 2002

In the aftermath of the September 11 massacre, most people of good will and judgment united in their condemnation of the perpetrators and their supporters. They even seemed to be united behind President Bush and the federal government for a bit.

But this unity could not last long. Now there are worries about government abuses, indiscriminate retaliation, and the unjust profiling of innocent people who just happen to look something like some of the perpetrators. These and related worries are leading America, the West, and all those appalled with the deed to begin to find themselves unsure about what to do next and who to trust with the task of finding out.

One of the main reasons is that government, as currently constituted, lacks trustworthiness. No matter how eloquent-sounding George W. Bush and Tony Blair and other officials manage to be as they speak to us about their plans and hopes, it is nearly impossible not to think about how these same folks or their standard-bearers have deceived us about so much in the past.

The famous or infamous exclamation, "No new taxes," from the elder George Bush says it all. Bill Clinton's prevarications lend it punctuation. And no one can forget tricky Dick Nixon, LBJ, and the others who have managed over the years to establish a reasonable ground for serious doubt about whatever we are told by the leaders of state in Washington and elsewhere.

Even today there is no consensus about whether FDR had early word about Pearl Harbor or whether some kind of selling out happened at Yalta. The instances could be multiplied infinitely. Be it at the most local, and up from there to the county, state, federal, and international levels of government, we find distrust all around us.

In many places police departments are nailed for joining in with criminals. Sometimes it is judges who get convicted for brutality and other gross indiscretions. The CIA is found to be out-and-out incompetent in its gathering of information and in its warnings to those who depend on it to manage our defense against foreign aggression. The FBI gets caught in cover-ups and gross misjudgment, and tax collectors are found to be bullying taxpayers beyond any justification. The Pentagon overcharges us all for some of the most elementary tools and appliances.

So when we live in times in which trusting our leaders is the only way to learn what is good diplomacy and needed military policy, how can this trust be achieved with the record government has built for itself? Is it any wonder that people are concerned even about the authenticity of the evidence against bin Laden? Is it surprising that once the patriotic feelings have subsided, people begin to wonder whether their honest grief may not be misused by their officials? When it is announced that this and that part of the economy needs large-scale subsidies, bailouts, and welfare, is it any wonder that many are distrustful and suspect that a great calamity is being used for the purpose of securing special privileges for some who can make their voices heard in Washington?

All this is because of a government out of control and

embarking on innumerable tasks that are none of its business, and repeatedly making phony excuses for doing so. All the pork the senators and members of Congress manage to extract from the Treasury surely cannot be for legitimate purposes. How much lying must be done on the floors of the House and Senate to make it all seem OK?

When that is the legacy of politics—indeed, when the word "politics" has simply come to be equated with shrewd power grabbing—how can a people unite behind their leaders and trust them when they say, "We know what to do, we know who to bomb, we know where to send your children to fight"? Can anyone be blamed for showing little trust in Bush and Blair and the rest, even though people may wish to trust them implicitly, rely on their goodwill and judgment in carrying out what needs to be done in the wake of the horrible assault on America and not just its own but other countries' innocent citizens?

I don't think so. The only remedy, in the end, is to make sure government does its duty and not all those things that must lead to its corruption. And what is that duty? To secure our rights, that is what. Sticking to the job description is a surefire way to gain the confidence of those one works for!

Liberty versus Democracy

Yuma (Arizona) Sun, January 11, 2003

Over the last several decades of American political life, the idea of liberty has taken a back seat to that of democracy. Liberty involves human beings governing themselves, being sovereign citizens, while democracy is a method by which decisions are reached within groups. In a just society, it is liberty that's primary. The entire point of law is to secure liberty for everyone, to make sure that the right of all to life, liberty, and the pursuit of happiness is protected from any agent bent on violating that right.

Democracy is but a byproduct of liberty. Because we are all supposed to be free to govern ourselves, whenever some issue of public policy faces us as citizens, we are all entitled to take part. Democratic government rests, in a free society, on the right of every person to take whatever actions are needed to influence public policy. Because freedom or liberty is primary, the scope of public policy and, thus, democracy in a just society is strictly limited. The reason is that government may not intrude on free men and women, even if a majority of their fellows decides to do so. If one is free, that is, a self-governing person, even the majority of one's fellows lack the authority to take over one's governance without one's consent.

This is what the Declaration of Independence means when it states that government derives its just powers from the consent of the governed. In a just society no one loses his or her authority for self-government without giving it up as a matter of choice. No one gets to operate on you, no matter how wise and competent he or she may be, without your giving your consent, and the same is true, in a just system, about imposing duties and obligations on people. They must agree to them. If they do not, they may not be ordered about. The only apparent exception is when it comes to laws that protect everyone's rights. One may be ordered not to kill, rob, rape, burglarize, or assault another person, even if one fails to consent to such an order. And when the job of protecting individual rights is done by government, government may order one to abstain from all such aggressive actions. But that doesn't actually involve intruding on people, only protecting everyone from intrusions.

It is along these lines that the idea of limited government arises: government may only act to protect rights, to impose the laws that achieve that goal, nothing more. Again, as the Declaration of Independence states, it is to secure our rights that governments are instituted, not for any other purpose. Of course, this idea of limited government hardly figures into considerations of public policy in the United States or elsewhere.

We have never actually confined government to this clearly limited, just purpose. It has always gone beyond that, and today its scope is nearly totalitarian, the very opposite of being limited. But there is no doubt that even though liberty has been nearly forgotten as an ideal of just government in America as well as elsewhere, democracy does remain something of an operational ideal. In this way liberty has been curtailed tremendously, mainly to the minor mat-

ter of everyone having a right to take part in public decision
making.

Though the original idea was that we were free in all
realms and democracy was concerned mainly with who
would administer the system of laws that protected our liberty, now the idea is that democracy addresses everything
in our lives, and the only liberty we have left is to take part
in the decision making about whatever is seen as a "public"
matter. One way this is evident is that many top universities
in the United States view public administration as a topic
having to do primarily with the way democracy works.
Indeed, since the demise of the Soviet Union, even though
the main issue should be the salvation of individual liberty,
the experts in academe who write and teach the rest of the
world about public administration are nearly all focused on
democracy, not liberty.

For example, the courses at America's premier public
administration graduate school, the John F. Kennedy
School of Government at Harvard University, focus mainly
on problems of democracy. At this institution nearly 40
percent of the students attending come from seventy-five
foreign countries, many of them from those that used to be
under Soviet rule, and what they focus on in nearly all their
courses is democracy, not liberty. Assignments in these
courses raise problems about implementing democratic
governance and leave the issue of how individual liberty
should be secured as practically irrelevant. Or to put it more
precisely, the liberty or human right that is of interest in
most of these courses is the liberty to take part in democratic
decision making. ("Human rights" has come to refer in most
of these courses and their texts mainly to the right to vote
and to take part in the political process!) Yes, of course, that

is a bit of genuine liberty that many people in the world have never enjoyed, so for them it is a significant matter, to be sure. But it is clearly not the liberty that the Declaration of Independence means when it affirms that we all have an unalienable right to life, liberty, and the pursuit of happiness.

The Declaration speaks of a very wide scope of individual liberty, while the premier public administration school of America teaches, at least by implication, that the only liberty of any importance is the liberty to take part in public policy determination. This, I submit, is a travesty. Once democracy is treated as the premier public value, with individual liberty cast to the side except for the right of taking part in democratic decision making, the scope of government is no longer limited in principle or practice.

Nearly anything can become a public policy issue, as long as some measure of democracy is involved in reaching decisions about it.

And that, in fact, turns out to be a serious threat to democracy itself. Because when democracy trumps liberty, democracy can destroy itself; the law can permit the democratically reached destruction of democracy itself! That is just what happened in the Weimar Republic, where a democratic election put Hitler in power and destroyed democracy. If you ever wonder why it is that public forums, including the Sunday TV magazine programs, the Op Ed pages of most newspapers, and the feature articles of most magazines do not discuss human liberty but fret mostly about democracy, this is the reason: the major educational institutions do not care much about liberty and have substituted a very limited version of it, democracy, as their primary concern. Once that is accomplished, individual liberty becomes defenseless.

Indeed, a democracy is just as capable of being totalitarian as a dictatorship is, only with democracy it seems less clearly unjust, because one little bit of liberty is still intact — the right to take part in the vote.

The Left's Strange Opposition to Preemptive War

Yuma (Arizona) Sun, February 15, 2003

It is a puzzle that so many people from the Left are opposed to a preemptive, preventive war against Iraq. After all, from the point of view of most leftists, it is perfectly justified to send in government thugs to prevent various evils in society.

Consider that all government regulations are preemptive measures. When government threatens to fine or jail someone for producing, say, pajamas that might catch fire, this is preemptive. There are no immediate, imminent dangers at hand. The pajamas may never catch on fire; they simply might—or there is some evidence that they could.

All the bans on smoking now being enacted across the country are similarly preventive measures—when a person smokes, he or she may risk seriously adverse health conditions. But that is not imminent, and yet thousands of politicians, especially those with left-wing leanings, insist that antismoking measures be carried out.

In the law these measures are also referred to as prior restraint—acting against persons or organizations (such as companies) before any harm has been done to anyone, before anyone's rights have been violated. In a bona fide free society, such legal measures are usually forbidden. That is the essence of limited government—it may not impose force unless acting defensively to protect the rights of citizens.

But statists of both the Left and Right do not want government to be so limited. They want it to act aggressively to prevent evils. Just think of the war on drugs or of vice squads arresting and jailing people who engage in peaceful activities, merely because something bad might arise. When defenders of the war on drugs say that even a little bit of indulgence can lead to bad things, and thus drugs should be banned; or when supporters of mandated affirmative action policies claim that unless they force institutions to deal with people in ways considered by the supporters of these policies to be socially proper, people may be disadvantaged—in all such instances, of which there are hundreds of thousands, the state is urged to act preemptively, to prevent possible but by no means imminent evils.

Yet, when the current administration in Washington, D.C., calls for preemptive war on Iraq, the very same folks who find the previous kinds of preventive aggression perfectly OK claim to be outraged. It reminds me of the hundreds of thousands who opposed the war in Vietnam and refused to pay their taxes because they disagreed with that government policy yet saw absolutely nothing wrong with taxing millions of people for other government projects that they eagerly championed but that the millions would not voluntarily fund.

The very idea that such statists on the Left consider it wrong to undertake a preemptive war must, therefore, be questioned. Is that really what they oppose? Or perhaps what they oppose is the United States going to war against Iraq? There wasn't a great deal of opposition to U.S. involvement in the Balkans not so long ago, for example. In that instance the enemy was not even so dangerous to the rest of the world—only to the people in its own region—as Iraq is today.

Something is amiss with the current peace movement.

Perhaps what irks so many on the Left is that the United States may benefit from being the country to get rid of yet another dictator in the world.

My own opposition to war with Iraq is straightforward: Unless it is demonstrated to me that there is a clear and present danger that Iraq is about to be aggressive toward the United States, there is no justification for a preemptive war against the country. It makes no difference whether Iraq is in defiance of the U.N. resolution that followed its defeat after the Gulf War. The issue is what justifies aggression against Iraq by the U.S. military, and that is the direct or the clear and present danger of its aggression against the United States, period.

But those who favor aggression against free people anywhere merely because they might do harm to someone, sometime, have no rational ground for opposing the current American administration's willingness to do the same kind of thing to Iraq, which has demonstrated not only that it has harmed millions of its own people but that it has made sustained preparation for war against neighboring countries and the United States, as well.

Indeed, conservative Republicans, who do not mind prior restraint—some even favor censorship—are more consistent here than are those on the Left who protest against President Bush's preemptive war plans. Most of them have never pretended to be against preventive aggression in principle, only if it doesn't work!

A Very Sad Perspective on Sexuality

Full Context (Michigan), June 1995

George F. Kennan was one of this nation's most interesting and controversial diplomats, the architect of the doctrine of Soviet containment, a doctrine he later argued against in favor of détente. As will happen with prominent people in their old age, Kennan has written something of an autobiography, perhaps more of a series of accounts and reflections about his life.

What is interesting about Kennan is that he is one of the few American diplomats who exhibit the flavor of the old American aristocracy. His style of life is reminiscent of what passes for an upper-class English stereotype: manners are nearly all. Civility, politeness, good form, and proper demeanor are uppermost in the minds of those who adhere to this kind of life.

The sadness of it comes through most poignantly in how Kennan views human sexuality. His reflection on this score bears lengthy quotation:

> There is no getting around it: we have to do here with a compulsion we share with the lowest and least attractive of the mammalian and reptile species. It invites most handsomely, and very often deserves, the ridicule, the furtive curiosity, and the commercial exploitation it receives. To highly sensitive people, it can become a never-ending source of embarrassment and humiliation, of pain to its immediate victims and to others, of misunderstandings, shame, and

remorse all around. Not for nothing do the resulting tragedies dominate so much of realistic as well as of romantic literature. Not for nothing has this urge earned the prominent place it takes in the religious rites of confession and prayers for forgiveness.

There is, in short, no escaping it: the sexual urge, the crude expression of nature's demand for the proliferation of the species, enriching, confusing, and tragedizing the human predicament as it does at every turn, must be regarded as a signal imperfection in man's equipment to lead life in the civilized context. It cannot be expected to be otherwise at any time in the foreseeable future. (George F. Kennan, *Man, The Cracked Vessel* [New York: W. W. Norton, 1993], 19–20.)

If there is anything the modern era may be achieving, it is the gradual abandonment of Kennan's view of human sexuality. This "yes, but" attitude toward sex has perhaps been the very source of our confusion and dismay about romance and sex.

For centuries human beings have, on the whole, accepted that they are caught between two parts of their nature, one that places them here on earth with the rest of the living world, the other which places them beyond the world, in some realm that stands above the world and shows the world's imperfections and shortcomings. Religion has popularized this vision, though it has been the substance of many secular philosophies as well—for example, the philosophy that Plato attributes to Socrates, perhaps the greatest teacher of Western civilization.

But whatever the source, this view has wrought havoc in our lives. Instead of seeing ourselves, including our sexual nature, as a normal, rational, sensible feature of reality, this view inclines us to view ourselves as fundamentally divided.

It leaves us agonizing about how to reconcile what, by its nature, cannot be reconciled.

In consequence, this view promotes cynicism, the abandonment of the effort to come to grips with our lives and solve our predicaments. If we are torn and if the division in our nature is indeed hopelessly irreconcilable, why bother to seek solutions? Why seek for the mean between extremes?

It was Aristotle, another great philosopher from ancient Greece, who began putting a solution on record, though his theories were lost to the West until the twelfth century. When Aristotle's more naturalistic philosophy was recovered, with the help of Saint Thomas Aquinas, it did serve to liberate science from the grip of fear and disdain. But it was not completely victorious. Instead the naturalist view, whereby human beings are the crown of nature, not apart from it, became fused with the earlier Platonic outlook that left us with a divided world and a divided self.

What did this do for human sexuality? It put us into a frame of mind that left some seeking to give it up altogether, against their nature, while leading others to debase themselves and abandon themselves to thoughtless, pointless, mad sexuality. The middle way was thought to be impossible. A sensible, rational, yet still celebratory view of human sexuality was left out of reach.

Human beings have been blinded, to some extent, by the sheer awesomeness of their life: to be thinking and self-aware is indeed nearly out of this world. It is almost forgivable that for centuries human beings didn't quite have a notion of where to place themselves and entertained the thought that they perhaps belonged apart from nature, at least in large measure.

But to have given this view the standing of our official

philosophy, such that even in 1993 an important figure in our society can unabashedly subscribe to it, is tragic. It perpetuates the misunderstanding, the agony — it gives little hope to our children, who may by this time in history expect a bit better on this score than we have been giving them up to now.

Clinton's Duplicity toward Women

Gaston Gazette (Gastonia, North Carolina), August 6, 1999

A favorite theme of those who champion women's liberation is that women do not need men to get through life. If the laws are removed that treat women as subservient to men, women will do just fine with all the challenges of life.

Bill Clinton and his wife, Hillary, have been riding on their reputation of being supportive of this feminist, women's liberation theme. They have insisted that it is their social philosophy, not that of the Neanderthal Republicans, that does women full justice.

In fact, however, Mr. Clinton has been repeatedly insulting to women. He just told us that the Republicans are against women because the Republicans aren't eager to give the entire surplus — and there is real question as to whether such a thing exists — to Medicare.

What really is Medicare? It is a forced redistribution scheme that has become a standard feature of the American welfare state. It collects money from people, at the point of a gun, in order to "take care of them" later in life. The assumption underlying it is that people aren't fit and wise and prudent enough to look out for themselves. So government must coerce them.

While Republicans do not disagree with this position strongly enough to have any effect on contemporary public policy, they want some of the supposed surplus given back to those from whom the funds were confiscated in the first place, rather than given all to Medicare. But why does Mr. Clinton want to give it all to Medicare?

Aside from the very likely reason, shared by many bureaucrats, that you never return money that you have garnered for your projects, regardless of how you garnered it, Bill Clinton says women aren't up to snuff when it comes to preparing for their old age. Presumably, if money is returned to them, they will waste it on something useless, say, go on shopping sprees. "You know how women are, don't you," Mr. Clinton tells us, in effect!

Well, women, in particular, are not wasteful with their money. So the government does not need to keep on in the role of a parent to them throughout their lives, indeed, at any time (since most already have parents when they need them). So when government has robbed them to the point that it is enjoying more than what it expected to get from this looting, the best thing to do is to return the loot.

At least Republicans see that this is the halfway decent thing to do. (They do not see that the completely decent thing to do would be not to take the money in the first place but to seriously reduce government's scope in our lives and charge people only for the basic features of a legal system. That is what government should be about, nothing else.) So they make a gesture toward the principle of private property rights—and support giving taxpayers back some of the money they have taken from them.

In this instance, the Republicans are at least not insulting women egregiously by proclaiming that government is especially needed to look after them. This is interesting because it is usually liberal Democrats who are credited with showing respect for women, for acknowledging their full emancipation. All the prominent feminists love Clinton because of how much more respect he supposedly shows for women. They even overlook his personal misconduct toward a young woman because, well, he is good for women's causes.

But here again what appears to be one thing is actually quite another. Bill Clinton's supposed respect for women is nothing of the kind. He once again is showing that he thinks them largely inept at dealing with life's problems. One such problem is, of course, reaching an age when medical needs will be greater, and one needs to prepare for this throughout one's life. Rather than counting on government to deal with one's medical needs, a grown-up, emancipated human being acts prudently and buys adequate insurance so as to manage his or her life competently even in old age.

But Bill Clinton does not recognize that this is what women can do. And he is turning to them not in their capacity as grown-up, responsible people but as another special interest group pining for government subsidies. No one can call this being respectful. And Republicans will miss out if they do not jump all over Clinton for this blatant pandering to the scared child in women, rather than showing women the proper respect for adult virtues.

Live and Let Live—
Everywhere

Orange County (California) Register, April 9, 2001

Back when I first came to the United States, I moved to Cleveland, Ohio, which then was the second largest Hungarian city in the world, second only to Budapest. Since I was intent on becoming an American, I strove with all my ingenuity to escape from Cleveland and the next year moved to Harrisburg, Pennsylvania, which was in no danger of being considered a Hungarian enclave. The idea that I should stay with Hungarian refugees after I had finally managed to get to the United States never appealed to me, quite the contrary. I was pleased, finally, to make a serious attempt to become an American, something that meant to me having certain values and attitudes, rather than being born in a particular place. Nor did I think that becoming American was an impossible task.

Even today I see one's identity as more a matter of what one believes and does than of where one comes from, one's color, ethnicity, and so forth. After all, those are not anything one can do much about, but who one is in terms of one's ideals, ideas, and projects is very much under one's own governance.

You can imagine my disappointment in recent decades with the trend in the United States that has elevated ethnic, racial, and sexual identity to great prominence. Who one is does not matter much, but what one is has gotten to be all-important. The recent census has developed a list of categories that would put to shame most of the old-fashioned racists who used to classify people by degrees of membership in some racial group. And this is finally having adverse consequences. People are beginning to resent being fitted into such categories by some bureaucrats who don't know them from Adam. In other words, there is afoot these days the stirrings of a second individualist revolution.

But not only that. It is now beginning to dawn on some folks that the politically correct ideal of diversity—which never means welcoming, let alone inviting, differing viewpoints on important issues but only having a wide array of colors, ethnic types, and so on, in the population in question (in other words, the diversity is confined to the shallowest kind, namely, how people look to others)—is against traditional community life.

In the Los Angeles area, for example, there are many close-knit communities of blacks, Hispanics, Vietnamese, Koreans, Chinese, Iranians, and so forth. Some of these communities have developed from the desire of newcomers to be near those who have been here a while and who possess an understanding of the newcomers' traditions, language, and culture. Just as my parents came to the United States and moved to Cleveland in the hope that they could get a foothold in a new country, where they would get help with their effort of acclimation and orientation, so millions of others who come to a country they believe is free from prejudice and class warfare nevertheless look for a community with whose members they have some things in common. And while this does not explain all the close-knit communities across the United States, it does explain quite a few of them.

The odd thing is that intellectual fashion now decries the communities that lack ethnic or racial diversity, even while the very same fashion embraces communitarianism, the view that membership in close-knit communities is most important to human life, in contrast to go-it-alone individuality. The conflict is clear: for some people, basing their community membership on race, ethnicity, national origin, shared culture, and the like makes good sense, at least for a while, though this does not sit so well with those who believe that communities must be racially, culturally, and otherwise integrated. In fact, however, not everyone fits some set picture that many intellectuals envision for us all.

In my case, I wanted a community when I came here, not the sort of community I had left but something quite new. Others had different plans. And in a free society one has a chance to follow one's convictions and not conform to those of some intellectual elite. Experimenting with different kinds of community life is one mark of a truly free society, and this is just what certain influential people consider undesirable. For them, we should all fit some pattern they have thought up as right for us all.

So today proper communities must have a certain configuration and no other, lest they offend the intellectual elites who like to tell us how best to live our lives. But the plans of these elites are repeatedly thwarted by common sense and human creativity. So for some time Asians and Hispanics will probably unite in close-knit communities (that some will fear are ghettoes), only to leave these communities eventually and become more integrated into America. I say, let a thousand flowers bloom, and let's not dictate to people the ways they can best flourish in their lives.

Never Mind One's Cultural "Identity"[*]

As far as I can recall, following my arrival in America I was intent on becoming American. It just felt like what I wanted to be. Except for some features of the country's politics, I didn't think about this as some higher calling but as a personal preference.

I had learned something about what being an American meant from reading a great deal of translated American pulp fiction, to tell the truth, not from listening to professors of American Studies (of which there hadn't been any back then, so far as I know). What seemed plain is that when one decides to live in a country, it is best to get acclimated, integrated, as much as that's possible. I didn't wish to sound like Zsa Zsa, that was for sure. So, I listened to popular disk jockeys in Cleveland instead of hanging out at Hungarian cafes where folks talked in heavy accents a great deal about the good old days back "home" before World War II.

When, more recently, it began to be fashionable to stress one's ethnic or cultural or racial identity, I was puzzled. To start with, what kind of identity is it that one acquires by accident? So, I was born in Budapest and heard a lot of gypsy music, ate paprika csirke and palacsinta. And, yes, I liked these things and still do. But how significant a part of me is there in that? My idea from early on was that what's important about one's identity is what one contributes to it oneself. Who one is shouldn't be a matter of happenstance but of purposive action. I liked to read and think about philosophy and religion, so if someone wanted to know who I was, I'd tell them about that. Or, in a less serious vein, about things I liked to do such as traveling and playing tennis. Some collage of these aspects of my life, of the things over which I have had some say, some choice, seems to me to make me who I am — not so much how tall I am or where I was born.

As I got to hear more and more about ethnic and racial pride, I was even more puzzled. How can someone be proud of being, say, Caucasian or black or gay or Asian? What had one to do with such things? Perhaps one might be glad of being tall or of having lived among other members of one's ethnic group if, indeed, this had amounted to a good experience. And one could certainly refuse to be ashamed of being black or white or whatever one could not help being. Even more, one might feel some affinity with others who were being picked on for attributes one shared with them and be willing, even, to unite with them to resist such treatment. But proud? Doesn't pride require some worthy achievement from oneself?

In my neighborhood newspaper, there is someone who writes mainly about Hispanics, and in nearly every column Hispanics are urged to feel special for being Hispanic. Why so? What is special about that? Doesn't feeling special for being Hispanic or Hungarian American or black or tall suggest that others aren't as special and worthy of feeling similarly about themselves? I have never liked the idea of a chosen people because it suggests that the universe or God picks some to be inherently, undeservedly superior to others. When I am told, "Hey there are some other people from Hungary you must meet," I respond, "Why exactly? Do they play tennis, love philosophy, or like the blues?"

The idea of ethnic or cultural pride, it seems to me, suggests something close to an insidious form of prejudice. Without having done anything worthwhile whatsoever one gets to be satisfied for belonging to a group. Just whom is one kidding anyway? (Maybe quite a lot of people, come to think of it, since there is a lot of this stuff going around.)

Don't get me wrong. There is much to be said for many cultural traditions that one can pick up simply by living in certain communities as opposed to others. (Of course there is a lot to be said against some of them as well!) All that's well and good—some of these things are indeed pleasant, delightful, entertaining, and so forth. But why should one feel proud? Surely, unless one has written some great Hungarian or Rumanian or Italian symphony or novel or poem or has otherwise made a valuable contribution to a culture, being proud of that culture is laying claim to something undeserved. (I have a hard time even saying "I am proud of what you have done" to my children—as if it were my, and not their, doing for which credit is due! Instead, I want to stress that I am very pleased with them, glad they have achieved a good thing. My kids may have been influenced by me, but their achievements are not mine, so I shouldn't pretend they are.)

I suspect that there is something rather sad behind all this collective pride. It is probably fear of being considered selfish if one simply prefers certain features of one culture over those of another, so one claims that these are collective accomplishments instead. Saying I will do something or enjoy it simply because I like it suggests that my likes should matter to me, and that's something widely discouraged. Who, after all, are you to do what you simply like? It has to be a superior thing for one to prefer it. Otherwise one should be fair and like everything equally well.

But this is silly. Each person has the right to assert his or her likes, tastes, preferences even if these have no special merit, even if they haven't been proven to outshine some alternative. Why? Because suiting oneself is a good thing. Surely if suiting others is commendable, suiting oneself must be also. And about this at least most of us have a clue, so I believe one should go for it without apology.

None of this means one has to attribute to these preferences something glorious, something especially worthwhile that will then pit one against others who prefer things of their own. Indeed, if simple individual preferences gained moral standing as far as they went, much of the acrimony among different cultures would perhaps subside. If you cannot unite behind some practice or tradition as being superior to that of others, if it really is just what some of us prefer as distinct from what others prefer, why fight about it?

Maybe, also, many people fail to take pride in their modest achievements, so they feel the need to attach themselves to the great achievements of members of their ethnic or cultural or racial group. But that breeds the clashes that have torn the world apart for centuries. I think a healthy dose of individualism can produce more modest ways of achieving self-satisfaction and sap us of the need to impose our ways on others who have different preferences. It's a bit like haircuts or favorite colors—they are pleasing but nothing to make a big deal about.

Beat-Them-to-a-Pulp Fiction

Orange County (California) Register, October 28, 2002

As an avid viewer of crime shows and courtroom dramas, I have noticed something insidious worth mentioning. It is far more hazardous to our way of life than all the sex and violence stuff so many folks bellyache about. I am talking about how the television and movie industries seem to find nothing at all objectionable about law enforcement people using threats of force to intimidate potential crime witnesses or informants.

Say that some cops think a restaurateur knows a thing or two about a murder victim or suspect, and they visit the place to ask questions. They are not getting the cooperation they believe they could and should be getting, so they start looking around for violations of health codes or of other government regulations. Or, again, suppose some émigré group member seems to the detectives or "crime scene investigators" to have knowledge of the whereabouts of a fellow member who may have done something illegal. So, no sooner do the wonderful officials see that there is a bit of reluctance about climbing into bed with the cops than they begin to drop hints about some kind of Immigration and Naturalization Service (INS) investigation.

I don't know about you, but this sort of behavior, coming from the "good guys" on television programs and in the movies, bothers me a lot. Call me a due-process fanatic, call me what you want, but depicting such tactics as perfectly OK is wrong.

No, I'm not one who believes that words or images can injure people. Yet, being something of a crafter of words myself, I realize that, of course, words have impact, as do images, stories, themes, and the rest of what makes up entertainment and even art. One need not believe that a movie's ideas force people to go out and follow those ideas in order to hold that such ideas can encourage us to see it as palatable to do certain things, to accept such things as OK.

The notion of a role model comes from this: someone is held up for admiration through the story line or characterization, and when such a person uses some strategy or method of solving a problem, pronto, this suggests that such a strategy or method is just fine, nothing to get bent out of shape about, even admirable. Indeed, all the emphasis on teaching kids the great literature of one's culture rests on the conviction that excellent novelists, for example, are going to have an effect on how people see the world, how they approach the problems they face in their lives.

Of course, there are those who go overboard with this and claim that words and images can injure just the same way as a blow to the face can. That is what spawned a string of court cases and similar efforts launched by radical feminists and hate-crime champions, people who, to use law professor Catherine MacKinnon's catchy book title, don't believe that it's "only words" when people talk ugly. They believe that images of women in magazines such as *Hustler* can't reasonably be taken to amount to harmless expression. They are weapons that need to be stopped with the use of police force!

No, that's too much, quite an overreach. Sticks and stones can hurt one's bones, but from words and images one can turn away—though that doesn't make words and images ineffectual, even entirely harmless. For example, I recall checking out that old cop show, *Miami Vice*, and finding it impossible to watch. Any time the star cops suspected someone of not so much illegal as bad conduct, they would rough that person up good and hard. No apologies, no self-doubt, no trepidation, nada. Simply charge in there, go at the suspect with violence, get what you want, and then walk away grinning with glee and happy as a lark. Being repeatedly exposed to this kind of thing will often produce complacency about civil liberties, at least when people look on uncritically and haven't a prior moral or political filter against such influences.

We have thousands of TV critics around the country, including many in my own community, writing for magazines and newspapers and appearing on TV, yet I rarely hear much lamentation about this misguided, albeit indirect, endorsement of law-enforcement malpractice. In the effort to keep our society free of official misconduct, it would certainly behoove us not to sit by and just accept it when the entertainment industry's star writers, directors, and actors make it seem perfectly OK for government officials to act like bullies, even if against unsavory, but as far as the story goes, innocent characters.

An Open Letter to My Children

Lincoln Review (Washington, D.C.), Spring–Summer 1994

Dearest kids:

You need to prepare for so many things in order to have just a reasonably contented life that I feel sad that I need to talk with you in a special way about the following topic.

As you know, I was born and raised in Hungary. Other members of your family, too, are descendants of recent emigrants from Europe. Your parents were not alive, and few of their parents were living in this country, when slavery and segregation were legal and practiced by many people who were white, as well as approved of by some who did not themselves practice segregation or hold slaves.

Nevertheless, in our day—and I am writing this in late 1992—some people believe that you and I are all responsible, in some measure, for slavery and segregation, neither of which you had anything to do with. Nor did your parents! None of us was guilty of perpetrating or supporting the evils of slavery and segregation. But these people do not care about this fact. They look at you and see that you are what they loosely call white or Caucasian and declare that you are guilty of racism.

Recently, a listener wrote to the National Public Radio (NPR) network about how he himself, who is white, is a racist—and NPR allowed him to read his letter for the entire country to hear. The listener used the phrase, "I am getting over my racism," as if racism were a disease from which he is recovering.

Even to honor such a remark by selecting it for broadcast is evidence of gross confusion. To begin with, simply being white can never make anyone a racist. Some sadly vicious or gutless people say such bizarre things, holding all whites collectively responsible for whatever ails nonwhites, be it as a result of racism or of anything else. But these accusations cannot be true. Why?

First, because if being white made one a racist, there would be nothing morally wrong with racism, any more than there is anything morally wrong with having curly hair because one is black or being sensitive to solar exposure because one is white. Whatever one cannot help being is something no one can be — and should ever permit oneself to feel — guilty for. This extends to being born to white or black parents or parents who are well off, or to being endowed with natural good looks or lacking them.

Whatever some people loudly proclaim, millions of whites in the United States of America not only had no hand in slavery or segregation laws but also had no relatives who did. The view that being white makes one guilty and deserves the imposition of various burdens is utterly false, not to mention a form of injustice identical to what racism amounts to. It is morally confused to hold someone guilty for being black or yellow or anything one cannot help being, and it is evil to make that confusion respectable.

I hope that when you think this through, it will be clear to you and you will never accept any opinion that identifies you as a racist only because you are white. If, of course, you have prejudices, irrational opinions either favorable or unfavorable to blacks or members of any other race or ethnic group, then you are a racist, and you deserve scorn and should feel guilt. But not for any other reason.

Moreover, don't be afraid to disagree with the members of a racial group different from the one you happen to belong to—even about issues involving them. You can fully evaluate their arguments, regardless of your or their skin color or ethnic or national origin. Such origins, race, or color make no one right or wrong—to think otherwise is indeed racist. To fail to air your disagreements with such people would often be a sign of disrespect. They should be as ready to handle your views as you are ready to handle theirs.

Here is another thing: It is hard to think of any person whose ancestors have not been victimized by some people. These, in turn, produced offspring who may well have benefited a bit from that oppression. To complain about that forever is pointless and perhaps even devious. It will, if continued and widespread, return us to prehistoric tribal barbarism—and the clannishness of the Mafia—in which the children of the children of the aggrieved had to mete out punishment to the children of the children of the transgressors. It was one of the noble achievements of the American founding fathers to have laid down principles of political justice in the Declaration of Independence that could guide us toward the ultimate rejection of such group-think human relations. Now, mostly at the hands of those who have revived group-think and collective guilt, America is being nudged away from the founders' conception of a decent society toward a state where all groups war against all other groups.

If one is not a racist—if one does not judge others by biological or genetic traits or characteristics over which they have no control—and judges others by the content of their character (to recall Martin Luther King's precise phrase), one should not sit still for the nonsensical racist lambasting unleashed these days by half-educated people. One should also realize that what lies behind the current racial strife is an ill-conceived effort to remedy past ills by way of group-think: affirmative action, the proportionate allocation by race of positions that require, instead, attention to competence, hiring and admission quotas, and so on. These ill-conceived policies have resulted in pitting groups united on trivial matters against other similar groups. They have also slowed down considerably the development of a racially and ethnically neutral culture in which what counts is how well one performs, not what racial, ethnic, or national group one happens to be from.

Of course, you will have your own ideas to offer about all this. But I, as your father, believe it is my responsibility to indicate to you clearly what I think about this matter, as I do about some others. That is partly what parents have to do—to educate their children about values. And justice is a value that is now being threatened in ways different from those that threatened and violated it in the past.

—Your loving Papa

5. Capitalism and Its Critics

Liberation or Imperialism?

Yuma (Arizona) Sun, March 29, 2003

One side says, "It's liberation"; the other says, "Its imperialism." Well, couldn't it be both?

During the heyday of the Soviet Union, its armies were always going about liberating places and people. When Nicaragua was run by a tyrannical regime taking its orders from the USSR, back in the 1980s, its leaders spoke incessantly about liberating the people there, even when this involved forcibly imposing on them countless measures they resisted.

Even in ordinary human relationships, say, between friends, it is often thought that imposing certain strictures on someone frees the person, really, so that all complaints are misplaced. Just think of the policy of intervention recommended to the friends and families of drug abusers! You coerce to set free! Or so the story is told, and when it comes to the war in Iraq, this can cause confusion for people.

Although in a given context the term "freedom" or "liberty" can be clear enough, there are several definitions of it that actually conflict. In one sense, for example, the intervention by friends of a drug abuser amounts to depriving the latter of liberty. That is the sense of "liberty" meaning acting on one's own judgment, following one's own choices, determining one's own actions whatever they may be. Those doing the intervention are depriving someone of liberty, of his or her freedom. But if one focuses on the goal of the

intervention, well, the story changes because forcing someone to stop abusing drugs can free that person to do many
far better things.

And if one thinks that millions of people are like the
drug abuser, carrying out a way of life that hinders true
progress, true flourishing, then perhaps one believes, also,
that they need the kind of liberation that will enable them
to do what they should, what will benefit them. That is just
how the Soviets saw it when they "liberated" the Czechs,
Hungarians, and all the rest by invading their countries and
occupying and nearly micromanaging them. They were
freeing the people of their ignorant way of life. The same
goes for the leaders of Nicaragua.

So, then, what is one to think about the liberation of
Iraq? It's a mixed bag, that one.

On the one hand, the rhetoric is about the freedom that
involves getting rid of other people trying to run one's life.
This is what George Bush is saying when he refers to how
after the war the people of Iraq will be free. The United
States will have liberated them from the clutches of Saddam
Hussein. On the other hand, though, many think the United
States wants to control Iraq, run it to conform to its own
priorities (such as the production of cheap oil), in which
case the liberation is akin to the sort the Soviets perfected.
Many Americans, such as entertainer Bill Maher, even
believe that people in Iraq just aren't up to running their
own lives, that they're incapable of democratic self-government. Their culture hasn't prepared them for this; their
religion is too much of a yoke around their necks. Thus,
maybe unintentionally, these Americans support interventionist liberation and support those who think Iraqis need
Americans and Brits teaching them proper politics.

It is important to know which sort of liberation is in fact

going on in Iraq. And that's not easy to do when a policy is as controversial as this one is, since those doing the arguing load their terms and do not always let us in on just what they mean by them. Those opposed to U.S. policy in Iraq have a stake in characterizing it as interventionist liberation, those for it have the opposite stake. And some obfuscate matters unintentionally.

We are left with the task of scrutinizing not just their terms but, often, their motives, which are awfully difficult to know for sure.

On "Giving Back
to the Community"

Orange County (California) Register, September 10, 2001

It has become increasingly popular for people in the business community to speak of "giving back to society" in the form of philanthropy. Bill Gates made use of the phrase when he came out against abolishing the death tax, but many other examples could be cited.

What is wrong with this idea anyway, if anything at all?

To begin with, when those in business make a profit, they aren't taking anything from society, so they don't need to give back a part of it. Yes, it is generous of them to support different causes with their wealth. Yes, it is often honorable to give to charities and other worthy causes.

But it is wrong to construe these gifts as "giving back." For when one makes a profit, one does so through a mutually beneficial exchange. One is not stealing something that needs to be returned.

Trade involves both parties giving up something to gain something else. One buys a pair of shoes, parting with money and gaining the shoes, while the shoe store parts with the shoes to gain the money. Both parties see this as being to their benefit; both see themselves as having gained in the exchange.

There are, of course, exceptions, as when trade occurs from thoughtless impulse or other kinds of imprudence. But even in such a situation the parties believe, for the moment at least, that they are benefiting, and it would be folly to interfere, thereby treating them as children rather than adults. Their mistakes will provide a good lesson, and perhaps next time more thought will enter into the exchange.

By propagating the idea that companies need to give back to the community, the idea is spread that the way they make money is somehow illegitimate, morally dubious, even underhanded. Is it really true that when Bill Gates makes his billions from selling his wares, he is ripping us off and, to do the right thing, must return some of his wealth? No. We have already gotten something back, right then when the sale was made. We provided the money for which we got the wares or services that we wanted, and the merchant got the price for these.

Sure, it is often valuable for companies or individuals to act charitably, generously, kindly, especially toward those in more, or less temporary, dire straits. And in some parts of the world, even here at home, there are people who are in pretty bad economic shape and can use the help that the well-to-do and successful are willing to provide. (More often than not, this is because free trade has been stymied there from time immemorial.)

But none of this is properly classified as giving something back, since nothing has been taken, at least when commerce is honest. But by making use of the language of "giving something back," it is suggested that the original means of getting the income and wealth wasn't, after all, quite up to snuff.

Are we then to take it that all those people in business who make use of this phrase have actually stolen things from the members of the community to whom they seem to feel they must give something back? If so, they ought to change their way of doing business and not get to the point where they need to return things to the community. If someone robs me and later comes to me to return some of what was taken, I have still been robbed. Indeed, I might have made very good use of the stolen stuff back when it was stolen. It is no good to give "something" back—all of it should be given back if that is how the wealth was obtained, plus some penalty for the original crime.

But in fact all the talk about giving something back is very likely a public relations ploy, meant to appease those who are basically suspicious of trade. Alternatively, it may be a way to try to make this awful capitalist phenomenon, making a profit, appear more acceptable to those hostile to the system.

Such PR stuff, however, does not accomplish the desired goal but simply reinforces the belief that, after all is said and done, business is bad; it's a way of ripping people off, and the "giving something back" ploy is meant mainly to obscure matters.

Unfortunately, even those who are very good at doing business—serve their customers well, run a good shop, pay employees handsomely—often think they aren't ethical, only clever or shrewd. This is partly because in much of our culture, the reputation of commerce is very bad. Business is often besmirched from both the Right and the Left. Many on the Right would have us believe that business distracts us from more important, spiritual things, while those on the Left think business prevents the realization of a fair and equal social order.

In such an ethical atmosphere, it is probably under- standable that people in business are twisting and turning to make themselves look good, even if it involves distorting the nature of the perfectly valuable, honorable work they do. To remedy matters, both those who do business and those who attempt to understand it need to realize that trade that is freely entered into, voluntary exchange, is a decent way for people who do not know each other personally to relate fruitfully to one another.

Why Islamists Detest America

Yuma (Arizona) Sun, April 19, 2003

Over the last several months, there's been a lot of conster-
nation about why so many Muslims detest America. Why
do they find the system of political economy associated with
the United States so objectionable?

Put bluntly, their charge that America's culture is "materialistic" is largely true, if by this they mean that people in
America pay a good deal of attention to how well they can
live, how much joy life can bring them—including when
they go shopping.

Not that Americans do not believe in God or don't
embrace some religious faith, but they do not do so with the
utter and blind devotion that leaders of the Islamic faith
demand of Muslims. For most of these leaders, the only
government that is legitimate is one that forces its citizens
to adhere fully to the Koran as the leaders interpret it. Nothing else will do, and when America associates politically or
economically with countries where this goes on or where
Muslim leaders want it to go on, the leaders believe the
association corrupts society, leads Muslims astray from the
Koran, which for them is a disaster. So these leaders hate
the country from which such influences emanate.

America, in contrast, rests on a classical liberal political
tradition in which tolerance reigns supreme as a principle
of human relationships. John Locke, the grandfather of the
American system of government, was also preoccupied with

figuring out how the government and church should be related. From his and some others' reflections, the American founders took away a liberal theory of government, one that opposes any union of church and state, especially in federal but now also in state government. This liberal theory has allowed a great many religious denominations to flourish in the United States—one needs only to look at all the different churches in one's own neighborhood to appreciate this.

Yet, Americans, in the main, confine their religion to Sundays or the Sabbath and during the rest of the week, they go about their personal and professional lives pretty much with little concern for how these activities square with their faith. Just compare the amount of public prayer Muslims practice to that of Americans!

Moreover, Christianity has by now made relative peace with commerce and the "materialism"—I'd prefer calling it "naturalism"—that Muslim leaders find so detestable. Christians see human beings as having a divided self, composed of spirit and of matter (soul and body), with both due some measure of care in one's life. The two sides do not always interact happily, of course, but that hasn't led to any great changes in American or other Western cultures.

Yes, commerce is often derided by writers, priests, ministers, intellectuals, and the rest, but this is recognized as somewhat paradoxical if not altogether inconsistent—after all, most of those doing the deriding are quite happy with the measure of material well-being they have managed to achieve, and few, if any, have taken any serious vows of poverty.

Finally, it is undeniable that a vigorous commercial culture is directed to living well here on earth rather than to preparing for everlasting salvation. We may not be able to take it with us, but we do like it a lot—material wealth—while we are dwelling here on Earth. And that probably does distract many of us from focusing on what religious leaders consider our spiritual needs and obligations.

The question is whether the Muslim leaders are right: is this freedom we enjoy in America and the West good for us all, or are we becoming decadent, shallow, and faithless as we enjoy our lives here on Earth? Unless we deal with this question, we will always be vulnerable to the harangue of Muslim leaders (as well as others) and will be detested by many Muslim faithful across the globe. And some of this detestation will be deadly at times.

But then perhaps that is to be expected when one holds up as an ideal a life in which men and women are free to choose to do not only what is right but also what is wrong. Perhaps we ought to be more confident and firm in our belief that this is how human beings ought to live. We ought also to stand up firmly in support of the system of politics and law that vigorously protects such a way of life. We should not hesitate to resist the aggression of those who find this so contemptible. They, after all, are mistaken in attempting to enforce by law the good life they demand of their faithful—simply no good can come from enforced goodness.

Indeed, if it is such a good life, why do they need all these laws to make people follow its principles?

Business Ethics Distortions

Yuma (Arizona) Sun, September 14, 2002

On September 9 the *Wall Street Journal* ran a sidebar titled "To Recruiters, Virtue Is No Virtue." It reported that people who recruit for businesses do not really care whether students take courses in business ethics. "Virtue isn't high on the list of qualities corporate recruiters seek in students." This is what was supposed to be revealed in a *Wall Street Journal*–Harris Interactive survey.

However, both the survey and the report are quite unreliable. It turns out that rather than asking about business ethics, the survey asks about "corporate citizenship." No wonder most who were interviewed seemed skeptical about the relevance of "ethics" to business education—the concept of "corporate citizenship" isn't the same as ethics and so is misguided and misleading.

If one asks an educator whether ethics has anything to do with preparing educators for their profession, the answer will naturally be, "Yes, sure, of course it does, just as ethics has to do with preparing for and practicing any decent, bona fide profession." But if you ask whether education has anything to do with school or university citizenship, educators could well be baffled. Does that relate to whether educators ought to follow the law? Or be involved in politics? Does it mean one must be a good citizen of one's country to be a good educator, regardless of what the laws are or of what politics are involved? What is meant, anyway, by such a loaded term as "corporate citizenship"? Business ethics is not about corporate citizenship, not if we consider the terms. Business is about guiding enterprises toward profitability, and ethics is about doing this conscientiously, decently, guided by sound ethical concepts.

People in business take an oath of office, as it were, when they go to work in their profession, and this commits them to being conscientious wealth-producers. In corporations, they sign up to care for the company's economic welfare, to make it prosper and fulfill its promise to produce conscientiously whatever it is that earns its revenue. That is where business ethics originates, from that promise, just as medical ethics comes from the doctor's promise to heal. Not that the ethics of human life in general does not apply, but even ethics does not commit one to treating one's profession as some kind of citizenship! Ethics requires one to be, among other things, honest, prudent, courageous, generous, and just.

Now if we asked people in business whether they take the promise involved in going into their profession seriously and whether schools of business ought to make clear that that indeed is the oath taken by business professionals, most would very likely answer, "of course." But "corporate citizenship" is a term no one would think of—what does it mean, anyway?

Students in business schools often face a very biased view of business ethics, for example, when they are asked about the social responsibility of corporate managers. Why "social" responsibility? Why not professional responsibility? After all, doctors, educators, scientists, and artists, to name just a few in other fields, do not talk about social responsibility. Sure, ethical business could include a social dimension, but that it does should not be presumed. Nor should decency and ethics in business people be equated with the choice to do pro bono work. The main issue is whether business professionals fulfill their promise to work hard and conscientiously at the tasks they assumed when they joined the profession.

Not that there is no debate about most of this. Some who reflect on the matter of the ethics of business professionals take it as given that such people are public servants, as are police officers, those who work in the Department of Justice, and members of the different branches of the armed forces, but this view is dubious. Professionals do promise, in effect, to serve those who come to them for service, who hire them. But they are not committed to involuntary servitude, to serve all who want what they have to offer. And they aren't public officials who must serve all citizens in society—all members of the public. If I haven't hired a broker, he or she owes me no advice. If I have no shares in a company, the managers have no responsibility to enhance my prosperity. But if I call the cops to help me cope with a crime, they owe me help simply because they are public servants.

Those who deny this adhere to what has come to be called the stakeholder—as opposed to the shareholder—theory of the ethical responsibility of corporate managers. If you own a little shop next to a branch of a company and the managers decide that it would be economical to close this branch, they must, by this outlook, consider your interests as one of their priorities, not just the shareholders' interests. Yet, this all rests on a view that denies a fundamental principle of business, that trade must be voluntary. The company managers did not volunteer to serve the little shop next to the branch that's to be shut down. They did volunteer to manage the company for its owners.

At one time, of course, all companies existed at the behest of the monarch and were, thus, public service institutions. Even the U.S. Constitution has some wording that suggests this: it treats the free flow of commerce as something that needs public support. In that, the constitution got it wrong—commerce, like religion or any other social project, exists because the members of society want it to exist, not because the government has decreed its value!

Consider, also, that few if any professionals outside of business are expected to do pro bono work in order to earn moral standing. Companies are routinely expected to make huge contributions to charities, universities, and international rescue missions. And they are expected to "give back" to their communities, as if they stole something from them! This is all utterly misguided, and unfair to boot.

In any case, whether business owes something to society and whether perhaps other professionals do as well are matters to be considered in a thorough exploration of professional and business ethics. These questions can't be decided by a survey and the findings laid down as axiomatic by some survey group and then reported by the *Wall Street Journal* uncritically—as if nothing problematic were contained in the finding that business recruiters don't much care about whether students in business schools take courses in "corporate citizenship." Perhaps they shouldn't. Perhaps recruiters and students really ought to care about being decent professionals in business, period.

Why I Am a Proud Market Fundamentalist

Yuma (Arizona) Sun, August 3, 2002

Freedom is often struggling to gain recognition, respect, and this is ever so true in the wake of corporate scandals. Though before we heard a lot from people about how freedom and free markets promoted greed, hedonism, and the "me generation," now some are denouncing freedom for being fundamentalist or purist, for refusing to be compromised or diluted with other systems, such as unrestrained democracy or vigorous government oversight.

Recently, the Congress has been urged from many corners to unleash a new wave of government regulations to tame the allegedly out-of-control, free-market capitalism that we've inherited from the era of Ronald Reagan and Margaret Thatcher. (Never mind that no such capitalism has ever existed anywhere!)

But what is at stake here, actually? To be fundamentalist, intransigent, or uncompromising about freedom is, recalling a well-known phrase from Barry Goldwater, no vice. Surely, abolitionists in the age of chattel slavery were fundamentalists because they refused to compromise their demand that slaves be set completely free, that it was not enough to just let them have some time off or otherwise moderate the extremes of slavery. No, the institution had to be abolished, period.

No less are defenders of freedom of the press, of artistic expression, or of religion fundamentalists about what they demand. No system of occasional, gentle censorship will do. Freedom must be absolute—only once a person has been convicted of a crime that violates the rights of others may such a person's liberty be taken away or reduced.

I am a market fundamentalist because I believe that each person is morally, and should be politically, sovereign and that business (as well as other kinds of) conduct must be free from interference unless something criminal warrants restraint. Anything else would be what most people in the press vigorously protest, being the fundamentalists they are—namely, prior restraint.

The fact is that market fundamentalism is simply a consistent demand for individual liberty, nothing more or less. It is now targeted as something bad because "fundamentalism" has been associated with terrorism and mindlessness. But, why not be a fundamentalist here? Why should democracy, for example, be allowed to limit our economic liberty? Who are these majorities, with some kind of mysterious moral authority, to force others to conform to various terms before they may carry on their commercial or economic activities? Isn't it the point of the famous example of the unruly lynch mob that a person may not be sent off to the gallows or otherwise limited in liberty unless it has been demonstrated, by due process, that he or she has forfeited the right to liberty?

The innumerable government regulations already on the books and now being proposed not only seem unable to wipe out occasional business malpractice but constitute a kind of democratic lynch-mob action, this time on the futile grounds of precaution or prevention. By that argument, the very idea of innocent until proven guilty could be tossed and the creeping totalitarianism of police states unleashed. (Moreover, proponents of this idea are naïve in holding that regulators are immune to corruption!)

If a system is in fact suited to community life, as the free market capitalist system is, then being fundamentalist about it, refusing to compromise its principles even from a sense of urgency to prevent misconduct, is the right approach to take. It is only thoughtless, stupid fundamentalism that is objectionable, when the fundamentals are accepted on blind faith. But in the history of economic life, it is obvious that freedom is not only more productive, more efficient than the alternative of government regulation and planning, but it is also more suited to human nature, which is creative and productive when not crushed by tyranny, be it of the democratic, monarchical, or single-party type.

In morality we tend to prize integrity, consistency, and consider those who compromise to be at least partly moral failures, and rightly so. Why, then, should we give up on this kind of fundamentalism—complete, unrelenting loyalty to sound principles—in the realm of political economy? No reason is given—by the likes of Professor Benjamin Barber of the University of Maryland, who tries so hard to substitute the regime of strong democracy for that of individual liberty—except that here the people who want to rule want to persuade us that upholding and championing a principled political system amounts to ideology, to being dogmatic, to failing to be flexible. One can only surmise that they do this in the hope that they can persuade some majority to do their bidding and rob us of the defense against such democratic tyranny.

Principles help people know how they ought to live and whether what others propose should be accepted or rejected. So, those who want to rule others don't much like principles.

Well, this trick is insulting and shouldn't be permitted to work. Market fundamentalism is simply being loyal to the principles of a free society, especially as they pertain to economics. Those who attempt to demean the free society are advocating political elitism where certain folks, maybe majorities, maybe demagogues, get to order the rest of us to do what they think is right.

I am urging that this scam be rejected in favor of, yes, unabashed market fundamentalism.

Wells Fargo
and the Press

Irvington-on-Hudson (New York) Freeman, September 1996

When in late January Wells Fargo Bank acquired First
Interstate Bank of California in what the press so gleefully
likes to call a hostile takeover, I was in California, driving
from one place to another for different speaking engage-
ments. So I had the opportunity to listen to many radio
news reports discussing the purchase. For example, I listened to KCBS-AM radio, the all-news station in San Francisco, on which this event was covered repeatedly over the
time I was driving north from Santa Barbara to the Bay Area.

Invariably, the reporters gave an account of this major
economic event in terms of how thousands of First Interstate employees will probably lose their jobs in Wells Fargo's efforts to consolidate its services and to secure a more
profitable operation for the resulting huge enterprise.
Employees were interviewed, and journalists as well as
expert commentators, pretending to some measure of economic and business expertise, gave their take on what
occurred.

In all instances they stressed just how this major buy-
out will hurt people, even consumers (because the reduction
in the work force surely isn't good for customers), just to
secure profits for Wells Fargo and First Interstate stockholders. Not one person advanced the idea that such a
merger would probably enable a great many of the Wells
Fargo and First Interstate stockholders to invest more

money in their children's education, clothing, health care, ballet lessons, and other efforts to give them a better life and that all this would very likely lead to more demand for labor, which eventually would directly or indirectly give those who leave the employ of First Interstate Bank another opportunity for productive employment.

None of this is certain, of course, but neither is it certain that those laid off because of the merger will not find work. Yet the media experts immediately focused on the possible downsides, not on anything worthwhile that might come of what had occurred. The one mention of benefit, namely, the possible profitability of the merger, came as a repeated snide aside, making clear that the experts thought of it as a crass, inhuman motive for doing such a terrible thing as consolidating two giant financial institutions. Profit making—which we should remember means achieving economic prosperity—was once again construed as some lowly aspect of human life, as some cancerous virus that only hurt people. This relic of Platonic political thought, whereby those who trade are of a lowly class, still governs much of the thinking of our intelligentsia.

Such narrow-mindedness seems to characterize nearly all news reporting, with only a few exceptions—in such outlets as the *Wall Street Journal*, *Investment Business Daily*, *Forbes*, and *Barron's*. If there were such a thing as a tradition of class-action malpractice suits initiated against the press, no doubt a very strong case could be made against all these reporters whose only aim seems to be to put down business and scare the hell out of the public, never mind their professional responsibility to honestly explore all the angles of their news stories.

What can be done about this? Well, it would be nice if business schools and other educational institutions made some effort to teach people who major in journalism a measure of economic wisdom. But that will not be enough, since economists typically try to avoid giving a moral defense of commerce and the free market. What is really needed is a moral education of the public, including the press, about how prosperity is a decent, honorable objective for people and how those who pursue it are doing the right thing. Is this going to happen soon in our educational system?

I doubt it.

Why No Protest over NPR/PBS?*

Over the years since I have arrived on the shores of the good old U.S. of A., I have never quite understood how Americans could tolerate what is evidently a government propaganda-broadcasting outfit, National Public Radio (and its TV equivalent, the Public Broadcasting Service).

Now and then I kid about how I am addicted to these, though it is not an addiction, rather a morbid fascination: I find it baffling that what is so typical of totalitarian systems could exist in a free society. The newspapers *Pravda* and *Izvestia* and their broadcast siblings were so much a part of the totalitarianism of the Soviet Union that they acquired a definitional status: where you find a government that has fully taken over the governance of the lives of its citizens, you must necessarily find the task of disseminating information squarely within that government's purview. In contrast, where the government is limited to the function of protecting the rights of citizens, such tasks as spreading the news, interviewing the best and brightest, and debating the crucial issues of the time are all left in the hands of the people through privately owned media.

Just look at the plain fact that the Constitution contains the First Amendment as the primary feature of its Bill of Rights. This amendment was considered by the framers of the American system of government as central to a free society, that no law might be enacted to empower government to mess with the press, so to speak. The idea that free men and women might have their thought and speech interfered with was thought to be, well, unthinkable. Journalism and religion, two realms among many in human life where thinking is of the utmost importance, had to be left free of any forcible intervention, lest the best part of our lives be corrupted.

In the rest of the world, in contrast, where the remnants of a political system in which the people are pawns and the government is master still persist, more or less vividly, the journalists and clergy are often in bed with the state. Great Britain, one of the countries that unleashed the ideals of human liberty about four hundred years ago, still has a state religion. Throughout a good many countries of Europe, Asia, and the rest of the world the media are substantially under government control.

But why here? How can a free society tolerate the network of radio and TV stations funded largely by tax dollars and managed centrally and with an evident and distinct political point of view? If citizens are free to think and say what they will, and government is prohibited from regulating their thinking and speaking, what is NPR doing taking the citizens' resources and diverting them to the propagation of ideas many citizens do not share, indeed vehemently oppose?

One of NPR's most evident ideological slants is that it loves everything government wants to do except what it really ought to be confined to doing, defending the nation with its military. Shortly after the recent flap over the collision between the American spy plane and the Chinese fighter pilot, NPR ran what I am sure its producers prided themselves was a courageous segment in which a bunch of "military skeptics" called into question the American government's version of that event. While NPR's several velvet-voiced commentators, interviewers, and announcers make no bones about how they love the welfare state and all those who champion it, these same folks project a distinctly antigovernment mindset when it comes to anything done abroad that smacks of defending America's security from those who might threaten it. Among the skeptics who raised questions about the official government version of this incident with the Chinese, several raised questions about the need for spying on China, even from international air space. This at a time when it is more and more evident that the government of the People's Republic of China conducts large-scale intelligence operations in the United States, wherever it can get away with them.

But the specifics here are not what's important. It is rather that we have what amounts to nothing less than a government-run broadcast medium, one that runs practically every university and college radio station's news division in the United States and which—though it admittedly has fine classical and jazz music programming—has carved a niche in American culture many people consider vital and indispensable. How can a free society have such a thing? How dare it?

And all this without even the slightest protest from those in our culture who are supposed to be the guardians of our liberties, our politicians, nor from those who would be expected to worry most about the evident threats a government-funded propaganda medium poses to the ethics of their own profession, our journalists. Not one politician nor any journalists appear to find anything amiss here.

Which is the most scary part of the story, as far as I am concerned.

The Cheerleaders of Envy

Orange County (California) Register, November 4, 1990

People who doubt the efficacy of ideas ought to consider how well liberal Democrats learned the lessons taught them by Professor John Kenneth Galbraith of Harvard University.

For decades now, and once again in his book *A Short History of Financial Euphoria* (New York: Whittle Books, 1993), the illustrious doctor of economic science repeats the myth that wealth is a matter of accident or, as he likes to call it, "good fortune," implying, of course, that those who possess wealth have no rightful claim to it at all. Consider these sentiments, as recently expressed by Galbraith in the *The New York Times*: "There is the tendency of the many who live in more modest circumstances to presume an exceptional mental aptitude in those who, however evanescently, are identified with wealth." He claims, quite arbitrarily and without even trying to prove his point, that "any individual, on becoming affluent, attributes his good fortune to his own superior acumen."

Not only have liberal Democrats learned Galbraith's doctrines well, they seem to have convinced a good part of the citizens of the United States of America of their truth, judging by how much headway the Democrats are making by bashing the rich.

The entire budget fiasco in the last several weeks was replete with indignant outcries about how unfair the advantages are that Reagan and Bush have bestowed on the wealthy, about how we need to slap greater and greater tax burdens on these nasty people in the upper income brackets, and about how the Democrats are only a little less saintly than Mother Teresa for their relentless championing of the poor and the middle class.

Yet these ideas promulgated by Galbraith, however well backed by his standing, are really quite lame if not outright fraudulent.

Some people do get wealth through luck, and often enough through political patronage. But is it not clear, after all, that when we work harder, consider carefully our options, make hard decisions, save and invest with foresight and intelligence, we are likely to reap more benefit than if we just throw around our labor and effort recklessly?

This is just common sense—it is evident in the simplest manifestations of human action. Drivers who pay attention to the road, who are careful and prudent, do not have as many accidents as those who drive recklessly. If I think reasonably carefully about what I write and put my ideas together with attention to what I am supposed to accomplish with my columns, they are likely to be published. If I just throw around some half-baked notions in a column, it probably won't be published. (Um, unless I'm John Kenneth Galbraith, that is.)

Is Galbraith seriously proposing that no correlation at all exists between economic and financial accomplishment and hard and smart work? Or is he capitalizing on some of those instances that are indeed accidental, whereby despite all the hard and smart work, a person meets with little success because of bad luck?

I am confident that the latter is the case. Surely even with Galbraith, a famous and not so badly paid employee of

Harvard University, some loose connection between achievement and position may be detected. While I have no admiration for Dr. Galbraith's economic ideas, he can at least be credited with the ability to produce volumes and volumes of alluring and erudite prose. No doubt, that is one reason why he is published much more prominently than I am, for example.

Would he simply write that off as nothing but my bad luck and his good luck? Would he not credit himself with at least some acumen—the ability to know what his public wishes him to say and to say that with some flair? Surely that is not without a bit of merit?

People who become wealthy—an objective that many people find crass only to the extent that it is not within their grasp—have, on the whole, figured out some things, including how to please other people, how to produce what other people would like to have at a low enough cost to reap a profit from the undertaking. That is surely not a negligible aptitude.

Entrepreneurs do not come into being from spontaneous creation. They need to think hard, practice, persist, and so on. Just because there are those wealthy folks whose wealth is the result of theft and looting—including government grants, subsidies, and other favors—it by no means follows that the honestly earned wealth of others does not deserve a measure of admiration.

But envy runs deep in the souls of unfortunately too many people. Fueled by a cultural climate that has never been very supportive of commerce—recall how the Jews have often been denigrated for being good at accumulating wealth—the envy that many feel against the wealthy is capitalized upon by the Galbraiths of the world, who concoct fancy theories that rationalize this envy into a righteous moral indignation that can be taken into the political arena by liberal Democrats and populists to win political power.

It would be nicer, would it not, if politics concerned itself not with such seamy matters but with how government can protect our individual rights to seek whatever objectives we can seek peacefully, be these wealth, education, art, or science. With cheerleaders of envy like Galbraith churning out their clever prose, that day is probably a long way off.

6. The Individual versus the State

The Myth of the Public Interest

Yuma (Arizona) Sun, November 16, 2002

One of the earliest topics I wrote about as a young man, a graduate student in philosophy, was the public interest. It even became part of my first book — but it made zero impact on public discourse, of that I am now convinced.

I saw something fishy in this concept back then, and nothing much has changed. I am still utterly skeptical whenever someone makes use of it, and there are innumerable occasions when it is invoked quite unabashedly despite my own and many others' efforts.

Recently, in my region of the world, a piece of land on the Pacific Coast came up for grabs, and various special groups and local and state officials got into the fray, arguing about what should be done with it. This was valuable property, which had been under government jurisdiction, but the government changed plans for some reason; thus a bunch of people (who had been permitted to live on it for very low rent) were suddenly disenfranchised, and the land then became a political football, with different groups hoping to get the privilege of making use of it. Of course, the usual political maneuvers ensued, and those seeking the use of the land tried to influence public officials to decide in their favor.

There is nothing very unusual about this process. It goes on everywhere that private property rights have systematically been violated and governments have confiscated property to use as they see fit, using whatever process happens to be in vogue to decide what "fit" is going to mean. But it is still amazing to me how utterly impervious to the call for honest, ethical communication all those involved in the process manage to be (all the while, of course, wagging their fingers when corporate managers engage in chicanery).

There is hardly anyone vying to have the power of eminent domain used in his or her behalf who does not claim that this will all be for the public interest. Be it a small stretch of coastline where some company wants to build condominiums or a resort hotel or a measure that will deprive owners of their right to develop their land—in all such instances and many more, those chiming in with their pitch are claiming that they have nothing but the public interest in mind.

What exactly is the public interest, anyway? It is the measure of what will be of value to all members of the public, period, as citizens. Members of the public are citizens in a community! All such people would have to be really benefited in their role as citizens for there to be a bona fide public interest at issue.

And that means that the public interest is something rather limited, since very, very few measures in society can benefit everyone in his or her role as a citizen. The American founders realized this and stated unequivocally that the function of government is to secure our rights, to, among other things, life, liberty, and the pursuit of happiness. So, the public interest, as the founders saw it, quite reasonably and rightly, amounts to having the basic rights of all citizens competently secured.

Which means that none of the claims made by different citizens, in their role as members of special groups, counts as seeking to promote the public interest. None.

It is only when groups, such as disenfranchised blacks, women, or others, cry out to have their basic human rights properly protected that some semblance of the public interest comes into view. Even there a lot of hokum is in play— as when groups claim as basic human rights provisions or entitlements to other people's work or income. No one can have a right to that—allowing such claims would amount to allowing involuntary servitude, or coercing people to work for others, which was supposed to be abolished along with serfdom and slavery.

Really, none of this is all that new—people have long made indecent efforts to cajole goods away from those to whom they properly belong by trying to hoodwink us all into thinking that this would be in the public interest. What warrants bringing it up once again is that there are so many people today who are outraged at corporate prevarications, and quite rightly, while perpetrating the lie that their own demands of government are all for the public interest. Let's face it, few, if any, folks resist the temptation to play footsie with the truth when seeking government largesse is involved.

Public Education Is a Bad Idea—for the 76354th Time!

Mises.org, March 7, 2001

In Tipton, Iowa, a teacher resigned because, reportedly, her superiors were about to reprimand her for allowing a student to do research on rapper Eminem. In Mishawaka, Indiana, more than a thousand students were reported to have walked out of school because they didn't welcome a nearly complete ban on music in response to a parent's complaint about lyrics in the Shaggy song "It Wasn't Me."

And in hundreds of places and more, the issue is basically the same: what some parents want from a primary or secondary education for their children isn't what other parents want. And, more important, what may well be right for some kids to do in school may not be right for others.

Yet parents are all taxed to support a system that delivers the same for all, albeit with periodic changes, based on the political winds. If the school board decides to ban research projects on someone who may be, for some of us, an obviously obnoxious performer, everyone in the district must abstain, never mind that they may find something worth studying in what the performer has produced. If the board bans certain books, movies, or music in the district, only the very wealthy will be able to escape this ban.

And if a new U.S. president gains office, he or she, too, will urge some nationwide policies, different from those of the previous president, that may help some but will usually not help all children in their educational goals.

To afford private education, one would need to be spared the confiscatory taxation that coerces us all to fund the public education that is imposed on most of us. Even those who do not pay property taxes directly, because, say, they rent, pay more rent because government hits up the owners of property for the loot, who then hand the cost down to their tenants. So there is no escape except for folks who are inordinately well-to-do or are willing to do without many of life's amenities to go it on their own. And even then, government officials force private schools to pass certain tests to qualify for certification.

Now it is true enough that nearly all young people ought to receive the basic tools that are usually provided in elementary and secondary schools. But then it is also true that nearly all young people ought to be clothed, fed, and given some moral education, something that is happening quite nicely, thank you, and thus far hasn't been taken over by the government. Why can we not do this when it comes to education? Why are children forced into the one-size-fits-all system of public schooling when this is completely antithetical to their nature as individuals having very different needs and contexts?

The result of the continuation of this policy is what we see around us day in and day out—battles over what policies schools should follow, who is to win and who is to lose when it comes to curricula, library materials, and prayer in school. It also leads to the constant vacillation of the one-size-fits-all system, depending on what band of politicians and bureaucrats happens to be in charge. Most recently, for example, in one Midwestern state evolution was demoted to a loose hypothesis in high school biology courses, only to have this policy revoked a year later when new board members were elected. And whether some measure of religious observance has a role in public schools is something of a political football throughout the country, with courts offering various rationalizations for having made several unrealistic rulings on the matter.

Yes, we all need education, as we all need nutrition, shelter, clothing, and hundreds of other things, and as parents we must provide these to our children—but not in identical shape or form. Those who grossly neglect to provide their kids with such basics can be made to answer for what they do—perhaps there should be a legal category we might call "parental malpractice." But handing the matter of educating kids over to the government is no different from handing over their religious training. It is a bad idea, and no manner of dodging that fact is going to do what is needed for the education of the young, certainly not President George W. Bush's twisted ideas of having government bring about the improvement of this fundamentally flawed system.

In many areas of life, people try to fix the symptoms rather than the cause because they are so wedded to certain basic but flawed approaches. These Band-Aid measures may serve the purpose of getting things to limp along for a while. And that is what is being done to America's primary and secondary education.

But what is needed is something quite drastic, even radical: let free men and women work to find solutions without recourse to the one thing government can do, namely, apply coercive force! That would unleash the creative energies of millions of people who are interested in educating children and who would then very likely find all sorts of ways in which kids could get the kind of education that is proper for them.

Not all would go swimmingly, of course. But very little is going swimmingly now, and everyone seems upset, hoping for the miracle of getting a fundamentally misguided approach upgraded. It is a futile hope.

Where's the ACLU Now?

Yuma (Arizona) Sun, October 19, 2002

Over the years the American Civil Liberties Union (ACLU) has taken up some causes that no liberty-loving American should belittle. Those accused of crimes should receive due process, not be railroaded toward a conviction. Those who aren't members of a certain faith shouldn't be bombarded with that faith's messages in public realms. And people not suspected of a crime shouldn't be treated as suspects, as some communitarians advocate who want to clean up neighborhoods at the expense of individual rights and due process.

But the ACLU is far from consistent in its defense of the Constitution. When it comes to professionals in the world of business, the ACLU is totally silent about these people's rights, about how government routinely violates them and fails to accord them due process. Here is how that works.

Business is heavily regulated in our society, and the modicum of deregulation is but a joke — usually accompanied by different measures whereby government keeps its hands meddling in business affairs. For example, the California energy market is said to have been deregulated, but this is a lie. At most, domestic energy prices are no longer set by government, yet regulations have not been removed from imported energy prices. The resulting distortions in the energy market are now well known. Yet, politicians and other power-seekers keep repeating the lie that deregulation is at the heart of the California energy crisis. Pure bunk.

The gist of the situation is that government sees itself as having the authority to micromanage business—set minimum wages, provide subsidies, set tariffs, and require inspection of facilities. A good case in point is the insistence of the Occupational Safety and Health Administration (OSHA) that businesses equip their offices and plants with numerous devices that supposedly protect the health and safety of employees and customers. Now this amounts to out-and-out prior restraint, treating the people in the industry as if they had no rights, as if their conduct could be restricted and their liberty curtailed, with no need to prove that they'd done anything wrong.

If people accused of a violent crime were treated this way, the ACLU would no doubt beat a path to their doors offering to help out, going public with charges of injustice against the government. Prior restraint is just that, limiting the liberty of someone before his or her guilt has been proven in line with the due process of law. The mere possibility of someone's or some company's doing something untoward in the market place is taken to be a justification for imposing restrictions on business practices. Indeed, such federal agencies as the OSHA, the Securities and Exchange Commission (SEC), and the National Labor Relations Board (NLRB) regularly treat people in the world of business as if they had been convicted of a crime for which the punishment was to have numerous financial and other burdens imposed.

With the fiasco at Enron, WorldCom, and other companies, where the strong suspicion of criminal conduct quickly worked its remedial magic, many people are asking that government impose added regulations and controls on businesses, just in case they are about to act illegally. Yet, where is the ACLU pointing out the fact that any such precautionary and preventive policy amounts to illegitimate prior restraint? Sure, the Constitution does authorize the federal government to regulate interstate commerce, but why is that taken to be sacrosanct? After all, the Constitution also authorized the southern states to uphold the institution of chattel slavery. Does that make that institution right, good, decent? Might it be better to recognize that the law is sometimes dead wrong and needs to be repaired? And isn't it the job of the ACLU to promote such repair when it is clear that the government is being intrusive and meddlesome?

I call upon the ACLU to stand up in defense of members of the business community and oppose government's regulating their conduct on the grounds that such regulation constitutes prior restraint, the very thing the ACLU has been opposing when it comes to the government's efforts to regulate the conduct of suspected criminals. Unless someone is convicted of a crime, government should stay out of the way and stick to the business of protecting us from criminals, not try to prevent people from perhaps becoming criminals.

It makes no difference how much people may worry that those in business will do something criminal or hurt someone; if wrongdoing hasn't been proven in a court of law, in line with the rules of evidence and other court procedures, then nothing may be done against such people. This is true even if they are wealthy and economically powerful. That is the restraint required of the government of a free society, however eager those may be who wish for a cleaner business environment. And isn't the ACLU supposed to be at the forefront pointing out all this?

Guilty before
Being Proven So

Yuma (Arizona) Sun, August 10, 2002

In contract law it is accepted that while one may be fined for failure to perform as one has contracted to perform, one may not be forced to perform. This is the rule against forcing specific performance.

In criminal law, moreover, due process requires that an accused person be convicted of a violation of a criminal statute before being treated as guilty.

It is also understood in much of the law, but especially in connection with the conduct of journalists, that no one may be coerced or punished until convicted — this is the ban on prior restraint.

Yet these same principles are largely rejected when it comes to the way government deals with many professions, especially business. We learn, for example, that just recently government regulators at the Securities and Exchange Commission (SEC) have gone after six investment banks, among them some of the biggest on Wall Street, forcing them, as the *New York Times* reported, "to pay as much as $10 million in penalties for not keeping email messages as required." The SEC officials, along with the National Association of Securities Dealers (NASD) and the New York Stock Exchange, were negotiating the fines to facilitate a settlement of concerns about the discarding of email messages at the banks in question. The fines were to be levied because government regulators found that these banks did not comply with rules about email.

Government regulators at the SEC point out, as the *Time* piece notes, that banks must preserve "all business communications they have sent—both internally and externally—for three years." And for about two years, "they must be kept in an easily accessible place." Because the banks didn't manage to produce all the email messages that regulators were expecting in line with the rules, they are subject to stiff penalties.

There is a perfectly sensible provision in the law that destroying evidence connected with a criminal investigation constitutes obstruction of justice, which is a crime. But what the banks are accused of is not this but of not following regulations. And it is here that the injustice should be obvious: the regulations that the government imposes force people to perform acts that are of considerable burden to them, without any proof, not even reasonable suspicion, that they have done anything wrong. Mere interest in these email messages, for example, can constitute a reason for forcing the banks to keep them on hand, even if there is no criminal investigation in progress.

Indeed, this points up one of the problems with government regulations: often they subvert justice by intruding in areas that should be the province of criminal law. For example, the SEC forbids insider trading. But frequently the issue is mislabeled. It isn't so much the use of information about financial matters unavailable to the general public that is condemned but the way that information has been obtained—stolen or used in defiance of fiduciary duty (the responsibility to reveal the information to clients who had a proprietary right to it by having contracted to gain it when it became available). Instead, those owing the information to their clients sometimes go ahead and use it first for themselves. And that should be considered a crime, though insider trading itself should not be since no one is wronged by it.

But government regulations confuse forcing a profession to follow cautionary standards with prohibiting criminal conduct. This is probably one of the main reasons that many who are regulated think there is little wrong with using whatever means they can, provided it is technically or plausibly legal, to dodge the regulations. They realize that they are being treated as guilty even though they do not deserve to be so treated, so they fight back with all their savvy. In the process they often skirt malpractice.

Not until this approach (involving what is basically prior restraint) to trying to make people conduct themselves sensibly, prudently, wisely is abandoned, will justice be well served in this area. If it is illegal, because unjust, to treat someone accused of a violent crime as guilty before proven so, why should this not apply to those in professions, including business, who aren't even suspected of criminal conduct?

Forced Paid Leave
Is Immoral

Yuma (Arizona) Sun, October 5, 2002

There is now a lot of joy, especially in California, among those who think that government ought to draw up the terms of their employment agreements, but this joy is misplaced. It comes at the expense of the principles of free trade in the labor market.

Of course, the labor market hasn't been free for decades in America, let alone elsewhere. The Department of Labor, the National Labor Relations Board, and other state and local government bodies have been dictating to trading parties in the United States how they must conduct themselves, how they must relate to one another in the workplace.

Still, unlike in many other countries, including most Western European ones, the terms of labor relations in America have been hammered out between labor organizations or individual employees and those who hire people to work for them. And that is as it should be: free men and women bargaining about who gets what from whom at what price! That's the basic rule of the free marketplace.

But the free marketplace remains intact only in a limited realm of the marketplace. Mostly it is consumers or customers who can still act freely, by either buying or not buying from vendors, as they choose. No one forces you to shop at Costco or WalMart or Albertson's; no one forces you to buy a Chevy or a Ford or a BMW or a bike or home insurance from this or that insurance company. That's still up to you.

Nor does any government force you to deal fairly—if you don't like your hairdresser's and dentist's politics or religion, you can fire—downsize—them and go elsewhere. This is where we are free, for better or worse. (Free people don't always behave well but often do, and it is difficult to tell which qualifies as one or the other from afar!)

But when it comes to producers, the intermediary employers—for the ultimate employer is the consumer—the government tells them all what to do, in greater or lesser detail. And in California, as in Germany, France, and other places where a "Third Way" economy is in force, firms must now provide paid vacations of a certain length, on the grounds that politicians know best. As Governor Gray Davis put it, "Californians should never have to make the choice between being good workers and good parents." He "knows," as all his fellow dictators in Sacramento seem to believe they do!

The trouble is, they are unlikely to know what terms are best in the employment relationship, and even if they did know, they ought to refuse to dictate these terms to others. They are not rulers, kings, or Ayatollahs but hired (elected) agents whose calling is to "secure our rights," nothing else.

The problem with criticizing the specifics of the new California law is that, of course, for some the law will be right; for others, an opportunity for abuse. Any such criticism assumes that everyone with a family ought to have the same amount of time off, something that is plainly false.

There are, for starters, too many people who have too many children that they should not be having at all when they cannot afford to rear them right. Such folks lead imprudent lives and subject their innocent offspring to their own misjudgment. These folks are not likely to attend to their families with their new longer time off, something they didn't earn but which was secured for them by political, coercive means. They are more likely to waste away their newfound hours doing anything but caring for their kids. At any rate, no one is in a position to tell for sure how many who get more paid leave now will do well or badly with this windfall.

But there is a general principle that everyone should know but which the new law violates: freedom of trade in the labor market. It treats both the employee and the employer as conscripted soldiers who can be ordered to do as the state demands. That is plainly immoral — it is entirely unbecoming in a government of free citizens. It is the mode of government of a dictatorship.

It is worth noting that reporters who claim the law "gives workers up to six weeks off" got it wrong, too. The law doesn't give — it takes from employers hours promised to them by workers and hands them back to the workers who didn't bargain for them fair and square.

Frankly, I have no special knowledge about whether most workers whom this law will affect should or should not have more time off. That benefit is exactly the sort of deal that employees should strike with employers and not have imposed on them from above. But I do wish that those who are the intended beneficiaries of such statist directives would refuse to take the "benefit" of such coercion and stick to their own voluntary tools for gaining the terms they want at their place of work.

Finally, it is generally conceded by economists that such laws hamper employment, even create widespread unemployment, by discouraging investment since the investors now must sign up for extra costs that aren't likely to produce any revenue for the firms they may start. This is just what is making Europe an employment basket case.

Government Internet Infelicities

Lima (Ohio) News, August 15, 1999

For the past several years, I have participated fairly vigorously in Internet communications. I have four or five different email addresses. I use one of the screen names on my daughter's AOL account. I send postings to webmasters of various sites. I am part of several discussion groups and fill out surveys on political issues. Often my columns are posted on the websites of such organizations as Bridge News, the Hoover Institution, and the Mises Institute, as well as on the websites of newspapers, magazines, and scholarly journals.

The Internet is a great place to communicate, although there are some aspects of it that aren't easily adjusted to. One hardly knows the people with whom one is in contact, and some of them surprise one with their curious mores and manners.

Usually folks remain polite even in the face of arguments on sensitive topics, but not always. Even those who take part in friendly chat-groups often resort to snide comments to achieve a kind of satisfaction that's difficult for me to fathom but must be of great importance to them. Yet that, too, has its uses: one can decide pretty quickly whether to continue communication with someone who is more interested in landing digs than in getting to the heart of an issue and resolving it in the best way.

In short, there is as much variety in human beings now on the Internet as there is variety in human beings, period.

Coping with it is a little easier than usual since one does not have to hang around to be abused, insulted, offended, and so forth. One's terms are easily insisted on, and the exit option can be exercised without any difficulty. Of course, despite the perfect conduciveness of this new medium to laissez-faire, government is eager to lay its hands on the Internet. President Clinton has been itching for some way to make government a major player here, and we all know of Al Gore's pathetic effort to inject himself into this sphere.

Just the other day Mr. Clinton issued an executive order that establishes a working group "to address unlawful conduct that involves the use of the Internet." This group will "prepare a report and recommendations concerning: (1) The extent to which existing Federal laws provide a sufficient basis for effective investigation and prosecution of unlawful conduct that involves the use of the Internet, such as the illegal sale of guns, explosives, controlled substances, and prescription drugs, as well as fraud and child pornography. (2) The extent to which new technology tools, capabilities, or legal authorities may be required for effective investigation and prosecution of unlawful conduct that involves the use of the Internet."

Interestingly, the one area where Mr. Clinton's intervention may well make sense — how government employees may or may not use the Internet — is not mentioned by the executive order, nor is the working group instructed to deal with it. That specific domain is in Clinton's proper authority to supervise, but instead, he wants the working group to advise on how to meddle with other people's business, how to behave like a vice squad.

In a recently posted column on www.mises.org, I mentioned that the government ought to be strictly limited to adjudicating disputes about rights violations. A few days later I received the following rather garbled message sent from the Federal Communications Commission public website ("fcc.gov"). From its tone, I concluded that it must have been sent by someone whose liberal democratic sentiments were simply bubbling over with excess passion. Here is part of what the message said:

> Hi: It's no wonder that you and your ilk teach at the 'Ludwig von Mises Institute' rather than a real institute of higher learning (does the Institute even exist apart from the Internet?), and that von Mises' work is not taken seriously by anyone with any sort of intellectual or professional competence, much less influence or real power. I am always amazed at the amount of right wing extremist crap one finds on the net, no doubt because the lonely, isolated, powerless proponents of this sort of paranoid crap have few if any other social outlets, apart from their isolated computer monitors. (I mean, what kind of a culturally illiterate philistine would be unable to see the good — whether characterized as private, public, social or individual — in having music programs in public school?) On a happier note, we can rest assured that none of the von Mises agenda will become reality, so long as our human world is recognizable as such, i.e., as it has evolved since approximately the enlightenment. God willing, the von Mises people will go the way of the neo-nazis, anti-semites, luddites, UFO-believers, and so on, ad nauseum, straight to the dustbin of history. Have a nice day.

I might as well tell you my response:

> It is not, I suppose, very amazing, after all, that you fire off a note without checking out any of your facts. First, I do not teach at the Ludwig von Mises Institute, I am an adjunct (unpaid) scholar. Second, I have taught in the California State University, University of California, and State University of New York systems as well as in several other institutions, including the U.S. Military Academy. Third, why are you so sure that such established institutions are better at

capturing the truth than those not funded by the government? For example, in the former the faculty isn't likely to
challenge the very basis of its own financial support, namely,
the institution of government. Just goes to show you how
reliable you folks in government are when you enter the fray.

In any event, it is somewhat scary to consider that here
is an employee of one of the most powerful regulatory agencies of the Federal Government firing off email messages
voicing statist convictions, thereby coming mighty close to
stepping outside the boundaries of his or her authority. Talk
about a chilling effect!

Maybe Mr. Clinton ought to do some housecleaning
before he gets set to wag his finger at the rest of us for how
we are making use of the Internet.

Why Not Just Force Them to Play?

Orange County (California) Register, September 1, 1994

Baseball isn't my sport. When they go on strike, I don't miss it at all. Nor is baseball a vital industry, as defined by those who like to talk that way. It is a sport, a game to be played, not really a profession.

But because in this society what people like has been held in high regard, because people's pleasures, preferences, desires, and enjoyments have been taken seriously, baseball is an important phenomenon. The fans have made it so. The customer is king.

This is no different from what makes rock and roll, the movies, much of television, and so on central to the life of our country. The people—at least many, many of them—want it to be so. In a free society that is what counts most, what people want, provided they respect the rights of other people to pursue their own ends in peace.

But many political thinkers would like to change this. For their money, if baseball takes resources away from, say, health services, which they believe to be more important—never mind what people want—baseball should be demoted. Thus, health services will be imposed as a priority, regardless of what people want.

This, indeed, is the message of those who put the opinions of the elite before those of the millions of people who support, among other things, the game of baseball. Job security, public parks, public television, old-age security, health and safety provisions on the job, and the like are supposed to be more important, and if people do not accept this, they will be made to comply. How? By means of legislation, majority rule, that's how.

The ideal of democracy, which is supposed to apply mainly to selecting the administrators of our system of justice, has been distorted to mean that by means of the political vote one can veto the choices, preferences, desires of millions of people. And the reason this is ridiculous can be detected by noticing that even baseball could be subjected to such democratic fascism, if only the politicians had the guts to suggest it.

Congress could vote into law a provision forcing the striking players and owners to accept certain terms and return to the game. They could argue, actually, that since the strike is putting some thirty thousand people, apart from the players, out of work—all those surrounding the game, from parking lot attendants to vendors in the parks—the strike is inhuman, a crime against the community, and the players and owners have no right to do such a thing. Just as the elitists argue that one should not spend resources on games when other vital tasks are underfunded, so the eager fans could argue that the game should not be stopped for the trivial purpose of settling differences of opinion.

In short, involuntary servitude could be instituted with the excuse that higher goals cannot be allowed to go neglected. There are, indeed, hundreds of prominent political thinkers, from the floors of Congress to the halls of academe, who reason exactly this way, at least when they can get away with it without stepping on the majority's toes. It would be instructive to remember the perversity of their thinking when involuntary servitude is urged on us—not related to a popular sport but to less widely shared concerns.

When Congress and the president want to spend money you and I have earned, fair and square, for, say, "social" projects that none of us has time to evaluate thoroughly, we should recall that doing so is no more justified than forcing baseball players or any other group of strikers to go back to work "for our sake." Indeed, it would help to remember that in the mid–nineteenth century the law permitted government to forbid strikes on just such grounds, namely, that it would harm the community. A judge in Massachusetts finally put a stop to this and asserted the individualist principle that workers may strike for any reason they choose. It is, after all, their own labor, not that of the government, which they elect to withdraw from commerce.

But back then the idea of involuntary servitude was anathema to the American spirit. That's one reason the Civil War was fought.

At Long Last, Prevailing Wisdom Challenged

Orange County (California) Register, April 25, 1994

I haven't had a hero for a long time, and suddenly I am elated. I have found one.

He is John Stossel, the ABC-TV news correspondent whose special program "Are We Scaring Ourselves to Death" on ABC-TV last Thursday made so many points I know need to be made in our country that I was overwhelmed. I don't know Stossel except from his various reports. I knew he was unusual when I saw a segment of *20/20* in which he allowed the late Roy Childs Jr., a libertarian wunderkind, to argue against special rights for fat people. (Roy was himself very overweight but had the integrity not to sacrifice his principles for any vested interest.)

Stossel must be one of journalism's few courageous professionals. He actually dared to challenge the prevailing wisdom about how risky it is to live in modern society. He showed that the main thing we have to fear is government trying to protect us from ourselves and from the fallout of modern civilization. Indeed, he went so far as to demonstrate beyond any reasonable doubt that the most hazardous, costly risk we face—one that kills more people than any other—is government regulation.

This is a brilliant point and one that is rarely made. Indeed, most journalists play along with government in its heated call for more bureaucratic meddling in our lives. And they try to scare us to death with their shoddy reporting of every crisis, as if the mere improvement of reporting demonstrated greater hazards for us all.

I am not holding my breath waiting for the next such demonstration of courage. I can see ABC-TV News being swamped with protests from bureaucrats—after all, their cushy jobs are at stake. And, no doubt, there are some sincere believers in the false threats to our safety and health.

Still, this is a sign of hope for me. Maybe this country, the beacon of liberty for the world thus far, can recover its concern for individual freedom and give up the mania about security, safety, and, most of all, government paternalism.

7. People and Encounters

Lincoln, Secession, and Slavery

Cato Institute Daily Commentary (Washington, D.C.), June 1, 2002

Over the last few years, I have become obsessed with a question: Was Abraham Lincoln a good American? By this I mean, was Honest Abe conducting his political life and, especially, his presidency in line with the principles of the Declaration of Independence? No, not the Constitution, although for many that is the major issue. But for me, what defines a good American is that he or she lives by the principles of the Declaration, by respecting the unalienable rights of all human beings to, among other things, life, liberty, and the pursuit of happiness. And as a politician, does such a person follow the Declaration's explicit statement that governments are instituted to secure our rights?

Lincoln made many statements that suggest he believed what the Declaration says, but he also initiated quite a few policies that suggest he was all too willing to compromise those principles. Consider the following clearly pro-Declaration statement from Lincoln: "The expression of that principle [political freedom], in our Declaration of Independence was most happy, and fortunate. Without this, as well as with it, we could have declared our independence of Great Britain; but without it, we could not, I think, have secured our free government, and consequent prosperity" (quoted by Harry V. Jaffa, *How to Think about the American Revolution*, 1978). Yet, Lincoln has a blemished record of following the ideal of free government in his political life, as when he issued this order on May 18, 1864: "You will take possession by military force, of the printing establishments of the New York World and Journal of Commerce . . . and prohibit any further publication thereof. . . . You are therefore commanded forthwith to arrest and imprison . . . the editors, proprietors and publishers of the aforementioned newspapers" (quoted by Dean Sprague, *Freedom under Lincoln* [Boston: Houghton Mifflin, 1965]).

Granted, one might believe that during a war there is little else a president and commander in chief can do but lay aside certain principles, such as the writ of habeas corpus, even the ideals of the First Amendment of the Constitution—which extended those of the Declaration, specifically, everyone's unalienable right to liberty, into the sphere of speech and worship. This is no slam dunk, however—perhaps those principles are so basic that they should never be compromised, even during war. It certainly looks as if Lincoln's fanatical belief in the union went against the Declaration's view of when people have the right to dissolve their government, a view he himself seems to have held at one time in his political career. As he said in January of 1848, "Any people anywhere, being inclined and having the power, have the right to rise up and shake off the existing government, and form a new one that suits them better" (Sprague, *Freedom under Lincoln*). So, what then is so sacred about the American union? Why cannot a substantial part of the population separate off from the country and go its own way? This is a good question, especially when we consider that Lincoln allows for secession on far flimsier grounds than does the Declaration, which requires "a long train of abuses and usurpations" that reduce a government to "absolute despotism," before tossing out the gang is justified!

Despite all this, there is that undeniable evil of slavery associated with the southern rebels, an evil that would appear to make a great deal of difference in deciding whether secession was justified. And many of the leaders of these rebels made no secret of their enthusiastic support for chattel slavery. They endorsed out-and-out racist ideas, to the effect that blacks were less than human and that whites had not just the authority but even the responsibility to hold them as slaves. Lincoln, oddly enough, shares some of these views, as when he said in his 1860 inaugural address: "I have no purpose, directly or indirectly, to interfere with the institution of slavery in the states where it exists. I believe I have no lawful right to do so, and I have no inclination to do so." And two years later, as the sitting president, Lincoln wrote: "My paramount object in this struggle is to save the Union, and is not either to save or to destroy slavery. If I could save the Union without freeing any slave I would do it; and if I could save it by freeing some and leaving others alone I would also do that. What I do about slavery, and the colored race, I do because I believe it helps to save the Union" (Letter to Horace Greeley, August 22, 1862). Then there is this, as well, from 1858: "I am not, nor ever have been, in favor of bringing about in any way the social and political equality of the white and black races. I am not, nor ever have been, in favor of making voters or jurors of Negroes, nor of qualifying them to hold office, nor to intermarry with white people. There is a physical difference between the white and black races, which I believe will forever forbid the two races living together on terms of social and political equality" (Sprague, *Freedom under Lincoln*).

Still, when it comes to endorsing the southern secession, it is not enough to point out Lincoln's failures in his position on slavery. Much more important is whether one group may leave a larger group which they have been part of, and in the process, take along unwilling third parties. The seceding group does not have that right, not by any stretch of the imagination. Putting it in straightforward terms, yes, a divorce (or, more broadly, the right of peaceful exit from a partnership) may not be denied to anyone unless—and this is a very big "unless"—those wanting to leave intend to take along hostages. Seceding from the American union could perhaps be entirely morally unobjectionable (if not perhaps prudent in all circumstances, because the union may be strong enough to repel enemies which the separated countries may not be capable of repelling). It isn't that significant whether it was legally objectionable because, after all, slavery itself was legally unobjectionable, yet something had to be done about it. And to ask the slaves to wait until the rest of the people slowly set about changing the Constitution seems to me obscene.

So, when one considers that the citizens of the union who intended to go their own way were in effect kidnapping millions of people, most of whom would rather have stayed with the union that held out some hope for their eventual liberation, the idea of secession no longer seems so innocent. And whatever Abraham Lincoln's motives were, however tyrannical his aspirations or ambitions may have been—either as feeble rationalizations or as serious, albeit misguided, convictions—when the situation of slavery is factored in, it is doubtful that one can justify secession by the southern states during Lincoln's leadership of the American union. Indeed, by the terms of the Declaration of Independence, secession is fully justified because everyone has the right to his or her life and liberty, so leaving a country with all of what belongs to one cannot be considered in any way morally objectionable. Even the Constitution could have been designed to make secession legally possible, akin to how modern marriage makes divorce possible.

Secession can be a sound idea—indeed, it comes under the principle of freedom of association, taken into the sphere of politics. It is a special case of the broader principle of individual sovereignty.

But secession cannot be justified when it is imposed on unwilling third parties, no matter what the ultimate motivation (in this instance, even if the reasons for seceding may have had little to do with slavery itself). Thus I conclude that, however flawed Lincoln was, he was a good American.

Which now leaves us with the odd and disturbing possibility that the American revolution may have had some improprieties, since the colonists who left England also took slaves with them. However, England didn't object to that, except to offer to free the slaves who would fight on its side. It had no offer on the table to abolish slavery in the colonies, so perhaps this is a moot issue, after all.

Margaret Thatcher, a Voice to Be Heard

Daily Objectivist website, July 25, 2000

For years I have been encountering nasty put-downs of this woman, mainly allegations about her being doctrinaire and stodgy, so it was with some eagerness that I attended a recent shindig at the Stanford University–based Hoover Institution on "War, Revolution and Peace," where the "Iron Lady" was to give the keynote address.

When you consider the impressive members of the Hoover team of scholars—Edward Teller, Milton Friedman, Thomas Sowell, Shelby Steele—little need be said on that score. Hoover has had F. A. Hayek, Alexander Solzhenitsyn, Aaron Director, and a good many other luminaries among its fellows, and now Lady Thatcher has been named an honorary fellow there.

As for me, I was selected as a national fellow for a year, early in my academic career, and returned recently as a research fellow and was subsequently asked to edit a series from their press, *Philosophic Reflections on a Free Society.* (For me it was like letting a child loose in a candy store!)

In any case, Lady Thatcher was not only a formidable presenter of her conservative ideals—in Paul Johnson's words, "open markets, vigorous debate and loyal alliances"—which veer more toward classical liberalism than to mere Tory traditionalism, but something of a hoot, as well.

First, here's a woman who minces no words in her praise

for Ronald Reagan and, especially, his foreign policy acumen, something rarely done by professors at institutions such as Stanford University. Although intellectuals love to ridicule Ronny, still, Mrs. Thatcher does not hedge her bets with them by downplaying her admiration for that American president, with his Hollywood associations and cowboy style, something I suspect he relished in part because it irked those academicians so much! Then, Thatcher does not hide from her critics but answers their exact criticisms (unlike many politicians who distort the critics before they then don't answer them). She takes them on frequently in her public speeches and essays which, by the way, aren't just a string of sound bites but offer up considerable fuel for thought on several fronts.

What stood out for me in her talk, however, is how delightful the woman is, mentally agile and quick on her feet, with sharp, to-the-point comments and a twinkle in her eyes.

Not too many politicians of age seventy-five would expose themselves to unedited questions from an audience of twelve hundred, after having been guided around for over an hour to meet the guests, and then give another hour-long talk of her own. Even fewer would respond to these questions with verve, humor, and extraordinary lucidity.

I won't try to summarize what Lady Thatcher told us except to say that she was foursquare in favor of liberty as against government regulation and regimentation. I might doubt the complete wisdom of her continued support of a very strong and ready American military. But I do join her campaign of spreading the Western values of individual liberty and political democracy around the world.

One may not find all of what she champions completely sound, but what stands out about this woman when comparing her with such people as George W. Bush and Albert Gore is her unabashed approval of unambiguous values. These are the ones that define Western classical liberalism—"free minds and free markets." (This phrase, by the way, adorns the cover of *Reason* magazine and was the title of an essay written by Edith Efron in the early 1970s. We decided to select it as the slogan for the magazine when I was still closely associated with it.)

It is not often that one can find anything halfway decent about politicians in our era. And, true, Mrs. Thatcher isn't an active politician any longer, so her words can more easily sound uncompromising. Yet, I recall that she has been attacked, as was Ronald Reagan, for her words apart from her deeds, and that because she didn't give quarter to those who kept soft-pedaling what the Soviet Union stood for. In many circles she is still not forgiven for that moral stance.

As a reader of the British press, I know Mrs. Thatcher has been repeatedly denounced by Social Democrats and Socialists for her confidence that a regime which preserves individual liberty will do far more for people than all the "feel your pain" masquerading of her opponents will do. Maybe those folks over there have forgotten all about John Locke, Adam Smith, and John Stuart Mill, the thinkers whose vision of society Mrs. Thatcher is determined to work tirelessly to realize around the globe.

A Medal of "Freedom" for John Kenneth Galbraith

Orange County (California) Register, August 15, 2000

It is a pretty good measure of how far we have come in America in our understanding of freedom from the ideas of the American founders that the medal of freedom was given to John Kenneth Galbraith on August 9, though he has been a stalwart champion of the very opposite idea of freedom from that laid out by those founders.

Galbraith, a professor emeritus at the department of economics at Harvard University and a fine writer and charming human being—so much so that William F. Buckley Jr. has been his longtime friend despite their deep political differences—has been a socialist for nearly all his career. He has been a relentless critic of capitalism and the market system, based on his essentially elitist and paternalistic idea of what governments must do for the people they serve—that is, make them all abide by tenets of fairness or, at least, his socialist version of that ideal.

Galbraith, though an avowed statist—not of the Marxist-Leninist but more of the democratic socialist variety—has been one of the most fervent bashers of the rich in contemporary American society. While not an explicit Marxist, he accepts the Marxist idea that capitalists create nothing and take a great deal that they should not be allowed to have. In his most popular book, *The Affluent Society*, he laid out a case for a powerful welfare state. He has written in some of the most prominent publications in our society, including the *New York Review of Books*, *New York Times*, *American Prospect*, *Dissent*, *Nation*, and so on.

One of his most well-known and widely studied legacies was created from a section of his book dealing with advertising. Here, Galbraith asserts that advertising is a device by which business creates desires in consumers that must be acted on and thus produce what he calls "the dependency effect." In other words, consumers become dependent on corporations because the latter create desires in them for the goods and services that corporations offer for sale. By this means, corporations become wealthy and make huge profits while resources are taken away from far more important projects—you guessed it, those the government wants to provide for us. The public sector is diminished, and the private sector unfairly benefits.

This famous section of *The Affluent Society* is reprinted in nearly all business ethics readers serving as textbooks for business school students across the world. Far fewer of these volumes offer the decisive rebuttal to Galbraith's position, penned by the great economist, the late F. A. Hayek. Hayek noted that Galbraith's claim is true but not just for business and advertisers but also for all human creative endeavors. The difference is that unlike Galbraith, Hayek did not believe that the desires that people may have for what is presented to them must be acted on. Instead, we have the freedom to choose whether to try to fulfill our desires, however they may be created. Advertising appeals to us but cannot make us do anything. It is a promotional project by which producers call out to us hoping we will consider what they have to offer and purchase it. But there is no guarantee at all that we will act as advertisers wish we would.

In what sense does Galbraith deserve a medal of freedom? Only in the sense that a certain conception of freedom does underlie his thinking. This freedom, which he calls "positive" freedom, is a condition in which people are given by the government, and at the expense of other people, what they can use to advance their lot. Such provisions "free" them to move forward.

The freedom of the American founders is different, backed by a different idea of human nature, one which recognizes that people in communities require first not to be thwarted in their efforts to make headway in life. One group of people will not conscript another group into involuntary servitude if the first group isn't thwarted by government and can thus provide what it needs on its own. Not equally rapidly, not to the same extent, perhaps, but if they apply themselves, they will flourish without coercing others.

Galbraith has never championed this "negative" freedom. So his views are alien to the American political tradition. It is not surprising, then, that he receives the medal of freedom from President Bill Clinton, someone who has done nothing at all to further freedom in this truly American sense.

To Galbraith's minor credit, however, he did, a few years ago, finally admit that capitalism is a far better economic system than socialism. He did this only in the wake of the collapse of the Soviet empire. And even then with great reservations and regret.

He was asked, in an interview published in Alitalia's October 1996 "in flight" magazine: "You spoke of the failure of socialism. Do you see this as a total failure, a counterproductive alternative?" He replies this way: "I'd make a distinction here. What failed was the entrepreneurial state, but it had some beneficial effect. I do not believe that there are any radical alternatives, but there are correctives. The only alternative, socialism, that is the alternative to the market economy, has failed. The market system is here to stay."

Al Gore, the Dixie Chicks, and Censorship

Yuma (Arizona) Sun, April 5, 2003

On March 31, 2003, Al Gore spoke to a college audience in Tennessee, claiming that the Dixie Chicks, a popular singing group, had been "made to feel unAmerican" and risked economic retaliation because of what they said. "Our democracy has taken a hit," he continued. "Our best protection is free and open debate."

Once again Al Gore, former vice president of the United States of America and Democratic presidential candidate in 2000, showed how little understanding he has of the American political system.

The simple fact is that when people speak out on issues, others who do not like what is said may decide not to associate with the speaker, in the sphere of commerce or elsewhere. Cesar Chavez, a famous labor activist in California, used to dispute the views of grape farmers and organized boycotts to protest, for example, the farmers' view of how much migrant workers should be paid, which was less than Chavez believed their labor was worth. The Dixie Chicks spoke out against President George W. Bush's policies and urged others to oppose them. One member of the group, Natalie Maines, declared to a London concert crowd that she was "ashamed the president of the United States is from Texas." Because of this they were criticized and experienced an adverse market response, including a minor boycott of their records and less airtime for their songs on several radio stations.

Now, in a free society one does not have to purchase products from those one does not like, even if this choice is for political or ideological reasons. The Dixie Chicks, for example, aren't legally owed an audience. Those who might become their customers may decide not to purchase their work, as is their right as free citizens. This is so even when the potential buyers are major corporations, radio stations, and the like.

None of this means that "our democracy has taken a hit." Indeed, it is quite the opposite. In a constitutional democracy people may either buy or not buy products for sale, may or may not patronize vendors, including producers of popular music.

But it is a blow to our democracy, one in which individuals have rights that even the majority is barred from violating, when government bans certain kinds of expression, be they political or even musical. It is this government intervention that amounts to censorship, not the refusal of free citizens to purchase products, whether newspapers, songs, novels, or whatever.

But Mr. Gore just doesn't get it. He regards it as an attack on democracy when people freely choose to boycott products they find objectionable, including products made by people whose politics others find objectionable. These boycotts are not censorship but freedom of choice.

Why is Gore so confused about this? It is because he does not see the difference between an economic boycott and a legal prohibition. But the difference is crucial.

People who exercise their right to refuse to purchase something from others, for whatever reason, do not force others to abstain from similar purchases. Economic power means using one's resources, large or small, to invest them as one sees fit, peacefully, with no power of the gun to back the decision. But when government bans some product, say marijuana, no one may purchase it. When government forbids certain expressions, everyone is forbidden to use them. Government, in short, wields legal power that should be used only to defend the rights of citizens. When it does anything else with its power, that power is no longer just.

We often hear it said that opposition to government programs that extort people's resources and use them in ways only some people want these resources used is itself violence to the intended beneficiaries. Governments pretend to be compassionate when they engage in such wealth redistribution. When private firms or individuals refuse to part with their resources for some favored purpose, this refusal has to be accepted in a free society, and resisted only by advocacy and persuasion, peacefully.

Since Mr. Gore seems unable to make the distinction, he construes the boycott of what the Dixie Chicks produce as an undemocratic, coercive activity. He couldn't be more wrong. But those on the Left, like Mr. Gore, take their lead from major socialist figures, like Karl Marx, who peddled the notion that when those with wealth did not help out the workers but insisted on paying them wages that were set by market forces—which means, the freely expressed wants of those in the marketplace—they were attacking the workers.

But that idea is misguided. When one legitimately owns one's resources, to withhold them or to part with only so much of them, and not more, is something one decides by one's own priorities. But, and here is the rub, the priorities of these market agents are considered irrelevant by socialists; to socialists, only what the government decides for us all counts as important.

Mr. Gore should rethink his warped notions. The Dixie Chicks are free to think and say what they will about Mr. Bush. But so are millions of others who dislike what the Dixie Chicks think and say, and decide to stay away from their wares. That is the only way one may protest the views and peaceful actions of other people in a free country.

Has Libertarianism Fallen?

Orange County (California) Register, May 7, 2002

Francis Fukuyama, the author of the famous book of prophesies, *The End of History and the Last Man* (New York: Free Press, 1992), penned an essay for the May 2, 2002 *Wall Street Journal,* "The Fall of the Libertarians," in which he makes several critical points, allegedly about this political outlook. I wish to address the more important ones.

Fukuyama labels Margaret Thatcher and Ronald Reagan "classical liberals." Just to clear up a misunderstanding on his part, these political leaders were in fact conservatives. The difference is that although both liked the free market because it yielded more goodies than the alternatives, both also wanted substantial control over personal behavior and favored more religion in public institutions (schools), hardly a classical liberal, let alone libertarian, stance. Ronald Reagan talked a good game about personal responsibility and freedom but then failed dismally to deregulate the market and mainly played the supply-side gambit, one that gives support to business to garner more taxes and thus make the government rich. This is not libertarian public policy, for sure.

The second point to note is Fukuyama's claim that libertarians are anarchists, which is just wrong. Libertarians are not all of one kind, of course — some are more anarchist, some less. For example, R. C. Hoiles, the original owner of Freedom Newspapers, was not an anarchist but came close, as did the former libertarian adviser at his company, the late Robert LeFevre. Many libertarians are far from anarchists. They do not believe that a government is necessarily evil but hold, instead, that once corrupted, a government (not a "state," as Fukuyama, in his Hegelian jargon, calls it) is more dangerous than any private institution that is corrupt! (Enron's collapse because of misconduct is far less hazardous to us all than when the feds go bad since the feds command guns, to put the matter squarely.)

Even libertarians who call themselves "anarchists" aren't really anarchists but believe in what we might call competitive government or the handling of dispute adjudications and law enforcement by private defense or justice agencies. That's not classical anarchism at all, which renounces all law and even defensive force (see, again, Robert LeFevre as one rather exceptional libertarian who didn't even believe in the morality of the defensive use of force).

Another related claim Fukuyama makes is that libertarianism is isolationist. Most libertarians, however, are not that but what we might call "defensivists." They hold that military or any other physical force must be defensive, or at most retaliatory, but never offensive and intrusive. The military of a free country is duty bound to "secure our rights," not gallivant about the globe, trying in typically futile fashion to right all wrongs. Things can get rather complicated, through mutual defense treaties and such, but the basic idea is that human beings should not use force against those who haven't initiated force against them, and this is as true of criminals as of aggressive governments.

Fukuyama then zeroes in on libertarians for advocating an essentially deregulationist approach to cloning and other forms of biotechnology. So what about the issue of cloning? True, libertarians look with great suspicion on government efforts to do the right thing in this or any other area where the issue isn't "securing our rights." Why is that a bad thing? Does government have such a sterling record righting other types of wrongs? No.

More substantively, libertarians also hold that once a new person has been cloned, his or her rights need respect and protection, and if provided with these, there should be no cause for alarm. Indeed, it is only in libertarian political theory that the cloned being would be seen as fully human and thus endowed with unalienable rights that governments are instituted to protect. A vigilant devotion to this task, in turn, would be far more just and safer than any large-scale government meddling in yet another area of social life that has no justifiable need for government regulation.

Sadly, Francis Fukuyama, who has done some respectable scholarship on many fronts, does a terrible job in this *Wall Street Journal* piece—he never mentions any libertarian by name, gives no quotations to back up his assertions about what libertarians believe, and just invents most of the claims he makes with no discernible support for any of it. So the essay is rather useless as a means of learning anything about a serious political alternative that people might find useful to consider as they formulate their political convictions. Fukuyama's piece, in other words, is a very bad example of punditry, approximating not even a modicum of scholarship. If Fukuyama is supposed to have shown that libertarianism has fallen—that is, failed as a good guide to public policy—he has botched the job royally. Unfortunately, his reputation may make it appear otherwise.

Yet discerning readers will probably spot just how ill-supported Fukuyama's points are and go on to read about libertarianism from a more responsible source.

The Courage and Wisdom of Shelby Steele

Orange County (California) Register, February 17, 2002

There are popular trends, fads, and the like in every culture, but the intellectuals—educators, theorists, critics, even pundits—are supposed to strive to be above those. Their oath of office is supposed to be "I will judge without prejudice, without trusting my mere gut reaction." And they are supposed to encourage the rest of us to spend some time being critical, too. This has been the calling of the intellectual since the time Socrates chose to die, rather than shut his mind to the truth in favor of received public opinion, back in ancient Greece.

Yet many intellectuals are by no means followers of this tradition. Instead they attach themselves to certain sentiments that rule their culture and that shut out dissidents. Sure, some matters are beyond the pale—a Nazi dissident is so obviously vicious that hearing him out would be too tolerant. Or a communist or racist.

But what of those who are fundamentally decent, indeed, extraordinarily intelligent and conscientious thinkers but who find themselves ostracized by an entrenched group who love their power and influence over people? Such a person is Professor Shelby Steele, the author of several incisive books on race relations in America, most recently, *A Dream Deferred: The Second Betrayal of Black Freedom in America* (New York: HarperCollins, 1999), in which he lays out a detailed argument showing that since the civil rights movement, much political activism intended to support black people has done blacks more harm than good. Indeed, he is rather blunt on the point that much of the legislation, embraced, sadly, by many widely published and paraded black leaders, has been insulting and condescending to blacks and has done little more than allay the guilt of many whites, making them feel they are being good people, rather than doing anyone much good.

Professor Steele was a featured speaker at Chapman University on Tuesday, February 15, 2002, with a merciless schedule in which he spoke to students and luncheon guests, took part in a panel discussion, and gave a public address. I was honored not only to meet finally someone whose work I have been following over the years, along with the work of those who are often intemperately critical of him, but also to introduce him to some of his audience at Chapman.

Unfortunately, the student group in the first audience was rather small, and only a few gained the benefit of his discussion of current American politics. The gist of his calmly laid-out and extremely well-spoken presentation— remarkable for its low-key and analytic, yet fascinating, tone and content—was that America is suffering from a schizophrenic disposition that is seriously affecting race relations and public policy. Using the term "triangulation," for which he gave credit to Washington operative Dick Morris, Steele noted that today politicians must all voice deference toward, and give license to, blacks and other minority groups.

Deference involves doing for them whatever they ask because, well, they have shamed nearly all white Americans for their alleged part in past and present racial injustice. The whites stand accused of, and many willingly buy into, the collective guilt syndrome and want to bail themselves out by supporting demeaning programs, such as mandated affirmative action, unconditional welfare, and even large-scale reparations (as advocated by Randall Robinson, in his book *The Debt, What America Owes to Blacks* [New York: Dutton, 1999]). License means not making any demands of blacks at all, exculpating them from nearly anything because, well, they are hopelessly injured and cannot help themselves. Such an attitude is not simply insulting but awfully damaging in our time. After all, while there may be pockets of racism around, there is no slavery or segregation, and with some self-confidence and the conviction that this is what must be done, millions of blacks could turn to helping themselves, to rising out of their dire straits, and to becoming competitive. Why not? Why should they not be capable of recovering from the damage the culture has inflicted on them? And why should they not now enter society on the terms laid out in the Declaration of Independence as basic principles, even though these principles weren't followed in other times for all citizens?

Those, however, who insist that what blacks need most is inducements to rise to levels of performance that enable them to compete effectively with others, are declared mean, even racist, and if they are themselves black, Uncle Toms. They have lost all sense of moral authority by now because, as Steele so poignantly noted, in our time what counts most is how much you care about social issues. (He noted that while Bill Clinton could get away with the Monica affair, had he been caught using the "n" word or something equally offensive, he wouldn't have lasted two weeks in office! Though in the 1950s just the opposite would have been the situation—adultery would bury you, but a bit of racism wouldn't even have been noticed. The puritan attitude has switched from the private to the social moral realm!)

Today, Steele went on to suggest, a politician must somehow have his feet in both camps—with those who stress deference and license as well as with those who stress the traditional values of hard work, self-sufficiency, sacrifice, and initiative. Americans haven't quite given up on these values, only repressed them because of the shame they have accepted for themselves for the past injustices done to blacks and others. So we have Bill Clinton parading as a "new democrat," being deferent toward blacks, giving them license, but also stressing, here and there, that they need to do stuff for themselves in order to recover and not wait for the whites, especially in government, to do it for them. And you have George W. Bush calling himself a compassionate conservative, still stressing the old values but making a big point of looking understanding, of accepting responsibility for the plight of minorities.

All in all—and there is much more to Professor Steele's ideas and presentation—Chapman University selected one of America's most stimulating, not to mention civilized and decent, intellectual dissidents to enlighten its students, faculty, and guests. One can only hope that some of what Professor Steele offered will take and have an effect that will help not just blacks but all Americans.

Time Is Not
Just Money

Yuma (Arizona) Sun, October 19, 2002

Over the years I've noticed that punctuality is treated as a minor virtue, at best, and even as an annoyance by many people. Entire regions of the globe seem to pride themselves on being regularly, routinely late.

Once when I was invited to give a presentation at a conference in Milan, Italy, I made sure I reached the place from Lugano, Switzerland, where I was living, at the announced start of the event, 9:30 A.M. Just for beginners, this was a bit late to start things off—at least from my experience, since in the United States morning sessions at conferences usually begin at 8:30 or 9:00.

I waited until 11:00, walking back and forth in front of the building where the conference was held, before anyone showed up. The organizers were astonished that I had arrived at the time stated in their invitation. I, needless to say, was astonished at their astonishment. I had thought that all those jokes about Italian trains running routinely late (Mussolini being credited with the solitary achievement of making them run on time) were, well, just jokes. But the Italians I have met keep telling me I should get used to it.

However, the practice of tardiness isn't confined to places abroad, by any means. My students over the thirty-odd years I have been teaching indulge in it with ease, I must say. Never mind that I keep imploring them to, please, at least notify me ahead of time if a paper will be handed in after it's due; never mind my begging that if a test is likely to be missed, please call me ahead of time. No, there are always slackers who ignore all this and are tardy and shocked that I am not merciful, not unless they have a really solid excuse (and having a funeral for dear departed grandma for the fifth time just won't work any longer).

Then there are those other cases that baffle me, when people in business say, "I'll call you back in five minutes," but the call never comes and you need to hunt them down yourself. Recently, I was trying to find a skilled service for a particularly difficult household task and answered some ads in our local newspaper. On one of these calls, I was told that the chief of the outfit would get back to me in five minutes. Alas, this was not a promise that was kept—the call came about twenty minutes later.

OK, OK, so what's the big deal? five minutes or twenty, why sweat about that? And why be concerned about keeping promises about time at all? Isn't that some sort of fetish, a sign of being obsessive, of being—well, you put the label to it, I am sure you've heard them all.

There are times when time is crucial—if I don't show up for my classes in time, I am breaching a professional promise, and my students let me know this by leaving after about ten minutes. If one doesn't show up at the doctor on time— never mind that doctors hardly ever turn up when they ask you to be there—your appointment is canceled and you may even be charged. (And no, I do not believe that every doctor who fails to meet a patient on time has an emergency on hand!) But there is also the problem that many people make promises they do not keep because, well, they want to please you. Those little white lies are motivated by the feeling that one doesn't wish to be the bearer of bad news—"I cannot call you back for a day or so," "I will not arrive until much later than you hoped I would," "I am not going to get the paper despite what you have asked me to do," and so on. These are akin to the white lies told when one asks how far something is down the road, and the answer comes back, "Oh, just a couple of blocks" when, in fact, it's close to twenty blocks one still needs to walk.

The thing that's most notable, though, about the vice of tardiness is that it shows lack of concern for one's word and for other people's plans. When I waited outside that Milan convention center, walking back and forth looking at my wrist watch, I was frustrated because I could have been doing something much more productive, and I kept having mean thoughts about the people who organized the event. Isn't this disincentive enough to get folks to become more punctual, to keep their word more vigilantly? I think it should be—but what do I know?

And then there is the money. All the tardiness around the globe may have rather impressive downsides, economically speaking, to say the least. So, while that's not all that's wrong with the lack of punctuality, it's part of it, yes.

The Death of a Little-Known Friend of Mine

Orange County (California) Register, October 6, 1996

I ran into him everywhere around Auburn. I used to joke about how he must be following me. He said no, it was me following him.

A couple of days ago he came to my office to say that he was considering taking my upper-division political philosophy class this fall. Then our department secretary told me he was looking for odd jobs. Would I have anything? And I had arranged to give him my library card, so he could pick up some books I needed for the next few weeks. He was a bit late, given his plan to be at the department around 11:00. It was 11:30.

Unexpectedly, Charlie, our department chairman, came to my office. He looked grim. "I have bad news, though not about you. Chris Young has died in a car crash. They found him only this morning. He must have run off the road."

I was stunned—I went cold inside, dead in a way. Although I had never had Chris in a class, he was a fixture around the philosophy department.

A 6-foot-6-inch boy—a bit dangerously overweight but recently dropping some forty pounds after he started running regularly and eating right—he was the picture of boyish innocence. His eyes shone bright, and he always had a hint of a warm smile. He was polite but light-hearted. He was a delight just to have around, never mind what you were doing or what he was doing. His presence always appeared to promise some joy in the air. He was like a merry bird about to bring forth some cheerful melody.

Cliff Perry, who teaches medical ethics and philosophy of law, worked with him a lot, preparing for the New Mexico bar exams. Chris was his sparring partner. They sat for hours in Cliff's office, Chris with the questions and Cliff struggling to get it right. On and on. Chris, too, was preparing for law school, so both were getting the most out of the exercise. I walked by often and usually said a brief hello, made some joke, mainly to acknowledge Chris because he was such a sheer plus, and I needed to affirm this.

And suddenly he is no more! As I am a father of three, with one already in college, driving back and forth from home on weekends, this terrified me. I couldn't shake the thought. What if one of mine died suddenly, without warning? I thought of Chris's parents and how horrible they must feel.

I was traveling later that day, and on the long flight from Atlanta to San Francisco, I was reading my last Laurie Colwin novel, *Shine On, Bright and Dangerous Object*, about a woman who had lost her husband in a reckless boating accident. This didn't serve to keep Chris's death out of my mind, although I wasn't sure I had wanted to keep it out actually. I felt he deserved to be thought of, often. Maybe that way he would still live somehow. (Aristotle said that immortality consists in remaining in the memories of others after one dies.)

I wanted to talk about Chris to my seat mate; but I felt I would be spreading the pain of his death, so I didn't. I wanted to call my children and tell them to be careful, not to take silly chances when they drive, never to take their eyes off the road or drive incautiously. But I felt that perhaps I was only trying to dump my own anxiety about losing Chris on other people. Yet why not? I realized that those who hadn't known him would not experience what I did, certainly not what those who were his intimates do now and will for quite some time. One cannot mourn without knowing the person; one cannot experience the loss of someone who is an abstraction to you.

So I decided to jot down some lines about Chris, as I am doing now. I know millions of people die every day, some of them catastrophically, tragically, too young. I am angry at those who talk away the loss of death by fabricating stories to soothe our sense of loss or fear of it. There is no way to make the death of a good youth acceptable. I was worried, however, that all I was doing was trying to find some way to help myself, in which case why drag others into it?

But in the end I don't care about some possibly hidden motive. I realize that I will not hurt others by trying to memorialize this young man who unbeknownst to him meant so much to me.

Chris Young was a delightful young man, a student of great promise and cheerful company. There is no way to make up for him. No substitution will do. All those who decry individualism should hold their tongues—it is the individual person, Chris Young, who is the being we mourn and miss. The reason we do this is that there is only one of him and his terrible death cannot be repaired by focusing on anything else. Those who knew him simply have to grieve. There is no escaping that.

.

8. America under Attack

Too Many 911 Calls?

Orange County (California) Register, September 18, 2001

I hesitate to jump right in with what occurs to me when horrible things happen like Tuesday's attacks on the East Coast. Several folks posed the question, however, "What is your response?" Now, finally, I do have more than the unprecedented emotional mess that was my first response, which included everything from anguish, sorrow for all those directly touched by the attack, to the deeply buried feelings I had as a kid when I experienced the outbreak, and then the rest, of World War II back in my native city, Budapest.

Of course, my first response was worry for the future of my kids and friends. I was holding my breath until I could make sure those close to me were OK, at least for the time being. Then my thoughts turned to what state of siege will emerge from all this! The rest of the day my heart was in my throat. Will Americans be feeling, henceforth, as we all felt in Europe back in the early 1940s?

Yet, as an academic political philosopher, I had to begin to try to sort things out—how should one make sense of something so monstrous? A couple of issues came to mind as I pondered all of it amid feelings of confusion, anger, impatience, and fury.

First of all, does this attack on the people of the United States possibly follow, somewhat naturally, from aspects of U.S. foreign policy? Not that any of it could justify the senseless, indiscriminate murder, but perhaps it could explain, in part, why those who are responsible, and their supporters, let their irrational hatred focus on the United States, specifically, the World Trade Center and Washington, D.C.? Or was this just what sometimes happens to good people, anywhere, when bad people, who are filled with unchecked envy and resentment and anger at some flaws in others, gain the upper hand—when they get hold of weapons and indulge themselves in the vicious ways they are wont to do, by wreaking utterly senseless havoc on the heads of anyone in their way whom they feel comfortable about hating?

What happened seems to me the result of a combination of the unmitigated viciousness of those who think in group-think and inflict their wrath on anyone, whether guilty of anything or not, who is a member of the hated group and of imprudent foreign interventions that have left the raging and vile enemies of the United States with something like an excuse for this massacre.

The idea that anyone working in private offices in New York's World Trade Center—or even at offices in Washington, D.C.—may be "punished" for what the terrorists allege is bad behavior by the U.S. government is outrageously evil. It pays no heed to such principles of civilization as due process and the rule of law. It employs the manners of raging beasts who have no patience with niceties, such as justice, fittingness, rights, and diplomacy.

That, by the way, is exactly why terrorism isn't the same thing as freedom fighting or resistance, which uses methods consistent with justice to gain freedom from, or retribution toward, a dictator or tyrant. Civilized warriors don't express their dismay, even outrage, by committing atrocities that they are supposedly protesting. Mass terrorists, people willing to massacre thousands, with no regard for the issue of guilt or innocence, have no compunction about flailing about violently.

So the first thing to consider when trying to explain what happened is that there are nasty, unabashedly vicious people who want to do rotten things to others, never mind guilt or innocence, never mind the rule of law and due process. There really are such folks, and in some parts of the world, they are in power and very well armed. Since their evident lack of serious attention to how to flourish in this life has left them with little to lose, they are reckless in a way that no productive, striving human being would normally be. None of the cultural relativism preached at our institutions of higher learning can obscure this evil.

Yet there is also something else to be considered. These deeds cannot be excused, but a relatively decent country's government can act more or less intelligently and prudently in the face of the clear evidence of violent viciousness around the globe. It's a bit like not going out on the street when violent gangs are on the loose.

For example, the proper military policy of the government of a just and free society should be to defend its citizens against aggression from abroad. In modern American military policy, however, the United States is following what a particularly disturbing bumper sticker announces about the U.S. Marines: "We are the 911 of the World."

Well, trying to be 911 to the world is grossly imprudent and a violation of the proper authority of the military of a free and just country. To order the American military to leave its post, literally, by forgoing its sworn duty to stand ready to defend the Constitution and the citizens of the country is not only dangerous but an abdication of duty—

as if one's bodyguard were sent off to rectify all altercations in the neighborhood.

Such a policy entangles the United States in dubious and muddled ethnic, cultural, national, civil, and racial conflicts across the globe. And when this intervention affects people who are already half-crazy with envy, resentment, and some legitimate grievances, it may be expected that they will act completely outside of moral and civilized standards.

However much one can sympathize with some who seek U.S. support in these conflicts, it is wrong for the United States government—funded by all the people's taxes and providing all the people's military protectors—to give it. (There are exceptions: for example, when the country receiving military aid is clear and unambiguous about sharing with us certain central values, such as the defense of individual rights. If we have a treaty with such a country, of which there are hardly any, extending military support can be justified.) Simply to gallop over to the Balkans or the Middle East or anywhere else, under the guise of helping NATO or the UN, to become the peacekeeper of the realm, is wrong.

These two factors together—the vicious resentment or envy of America's great success and the mindless response to America's meddlesome military adventurism—have, I believe, produced the horrible deeds Americans experienced and watched all through the morning of September 11, 2001.

It will take years to come to terms with what happened. The families of those who were killed will be nearly immobilized from sorrow and pain, as will many others who have the capacity for compassion. But perhaps one slight silver lining could arise from this atrocity.

Maybe instead of spending tax funds on zillions of matters that are none of its business, our government will begin to recall the reason for its existence, "to secure (our) rights," rather than parade about and serve as the vice squad of the globe. Diverting funds to subsidize all sorts of tasks, worthy and unworthy, has left the proper functions of the intelligence and military communities without sufficient support.

Once this is rectified, then perhaps the task of defending our rights, on all the intricate fronts where that's needed, will be carried out in ways that might even prevent most terrorism in the future. But if government continues to be the Santa Claus of every pet project for every special interest group, its proper task of protecting the rights of its citizens will continue to be underfunded and neglected.

Hate Crimes and
bin Laden's Gang*

Many people, especially those on campuses across the country, are concerned that retaliation may be made not only against those responsible for the September 11 massacre but also against those who harbor the perpetrators, who provide support to them, or who may be near them when a retaliatory measure is taken. I share some of these concerns, mainly the last, because innocent people should not be made to suffer for the viciousness of others.

I do, however, have a problem with the sincerity of this concern, when expressed by people who are, in another context, very eager to punish not just those who engage in what are called hate crimes but also those who spread hate — for example, by inflammatory speech or pamphleteering — without actually committing a physical assault.

Among those urging such punitive measures are the folks at the Southern Poverty Law Center in Montgomery, Alabama, who propose legal action against those who spread hate but do not engage in aggressive action against anyone. Morris Dees, the very popular leader of this organization, is famous for carrying out one of the Center's main missions, to "battle hate groups whose followers have violated the rights of others." They argue that such groups spread hate and induce gullible folks to commit crimes, and they believe that at least wrongful death law suits should be directed at such folks when those who are influenced by them commit murder. If memory serves me right, they also urge criminal prosecution of such hatemongers.

Now if I am not mistaken, spreading hate is something quite a few people across the globe do. And certainly some of this hate is directed against Americans, especially those among Americans who engage in business. Indeed, who could doubt this now? Osama bin Laden and his cohorts are certainly spreading hate toward Americans, in fact toward all those who embrace the values associated with America, such as individualism—in the form of defending our unalienable individual rights—capitalism, commercialism, and the unabashed pursuit of happiness here on earth.

Now, it seems to me that if the campaign against hate crimes is justified here in America, something similar against all those who spread such hate against Americans and other Westerners—or anyone, for that matter—would also be justified. In short, pacifism isn't the right answer, as Mr. Dees certainly makes clear by his speeches and actions. Neither he nor his many supporters in the intellectual community believe that we should do nothing about, or be loving toward, those who spread hate. They believe, quite the contrary, that such people should be severely punished, even sent to jail.

So it seems, when it comes to hating some people, the answer to the problem—for many right-minded intellectuals—isn't love and understanding and turning the other cheek but firm punitive action! Yet, it seems, when such promulgation of hate goes on against stock and bond sellers, capitalists, and other completely innocent people who are the usual victims of terrorism, this hatemongering does not qualify for a harsh, merciless response.

Granted, the haters in these instances live outside the jurisdiction of American law. Yet their deeds are not different from the crimes committed by those influenced by domestic hatemongers.

Indeed, judging by the complete disregard these hatemongers have for innocent people, the indignation with their ideas and conduct should be far more intense than it is for the few domestic perpetrators of similar acts. So it would seem that the very same folks who are urging—and funding—Dees and his colleagues would eagerly urge our government to take action against the foreign haters and those who carry this hate into terrorist deeds against Americans and others whom they attack to make their point. One would suppose that retaliatory military action would be favored by such enemies of hate.

Alas, it does not seem so. Hating blacks, Jews, gays, and so on is not just vile and vicious but deserves forceful retaliation, from Dees' and his supporters' point of view. So why not retaliate against those who hate Americans, Jews, capitalists, and so on, only this time from abroad?

Maybe consistency is not a great virtue—Emerson has told us that a foolish consistency is the hobgoblin of little minds. But perhaps this is not about foolish consistency but rather about integrity. Those who are perfectly willing to retaliate against the perpetrators of domestic hate crimes would, I believe, show integrity if they demanded the same treatment for those abroad who hate Americans.

Government, Liberty, and Security

Yuma (Arizona) Sun, January 4, 2003

In the wake of recent concerns about terrorism, there has developed yet another controversy about the scope and size of government's role in society. The idea that liberty should be sacrificed to meet the challenge of security against terrorism has been widely encouraged by polls that pose the issue in terms such as: "Do you prefer greater security against terrorism even if it means the loss of liberty?" And often the answer to such a question is "yes." But that is because people are presented with false alternatives.

It is true that as long as a great many areas of society are under the control of government, when threatening situations arise, government will take up the task, often rather eagerly, of providing security. This means that in many public places, such as roads, parks, schools, airports, court houses, and so on the authorities will adopt inspection and search policies that appear to be a clear threat to our liberties. Rather than being able to just hop a plane after parking one's car, now one has to have the car inspected by some gendarme before it can be parked, stand in a long line and have all one's luggage scrutinized, and then often submit to random searches by, you guessed it, government agents. This sure looks as if liberty is taking a serious beating in favor of increased security.

But there is a mistake here. If I enter a bank and have to go through different security measures carried out by private guards, this isn't an infringement of my liberty. Those who own the bank have the right to adopt security measures, great or small, to their heart's content. If I don't want to submit to them, I can either find another bank without such stringent security measures or avoid going to banks altogether. I am quite free, but so is the bank. So the bank's insistence on greater security is actually an exercise of its owners' liberty!

In my house, I may be paranoid enough to require people who visit me to empty their pockets and demonstrate their harmlessness in various ways. No one's liberty is infringed by that since no one has a right to be in my house without my permission. It may not be very pleasant to meet my terms when visiting me, but that hasn't got anything to do with the sacrifice of liberty for security.

The trouble lies not with increasing needed security measures but in having this done by the government in realms where the government hasn't any business operating. Why are government officials at airports? Airports have nothing to do with securing our rights, upholding justice, or other legitimate legal affairs. Airports are, in fact, no different from coffee houses or playgrounds or indeed any other place of private business. People seek a service and are provided with it on certain terms. In times of terrorist or other threats, even impending natural ones, the terms may become more cumbersome. But that is as it should be. If there is an increase in burglaries in my neighborhood, I will be more careful about letting people enter my home — I will check them out, ask them to identify themselves, and so forth. None of this violates their rights.

It is only when government gets into the act of providing the needed security, apart from protecting our rights, that the issue of rights violation arises. This is because government is supposed to be in the business of protecting our rights, so when it worries too much about other kinds of security, and in the process, subjects citizens to all kinds of scrutiny, it seems that government has switched roles. Rather than protecting us from violations of our rights, government is now engaged in just the activities that are considered, normally, to be rights violations. Random searches by government agents of citizens who haven't done anything to deserve this treatment are completely unseemly in a free society. Except that government has usurped so many areas of social life—schools, transportation, athletics, and so forth—that it is nearly omnipresent with its meddling ways.

When government takes charge of all these areas of our life, it becomes a bully, even though the same efforts made by private parties would be quite acceptable. IBM or K-Mart or even a grocery store could install preemptive security devices, and no one in his right mind would construe that as a sign of tyranny or as a violation of anyone's rights. It is, after all, their own realm they would be taking care of.

And usually there are alternatives to turn to, where different means of providing preemptive security are used, so one doesn't have to comply with IBM, K-Mart, or the grocery store with the draconian security measures. When, however, government adopts these measures, they do seem tyrannical because government may not use prior restraint—that is, preemptive measures, such as random searches—and because government has monopoly powers in all public places.

Anti-Americanism
Isn't Unusual*

For those who were utterly surprised by September 11, 2001, it may be useful to recall that America has always been hated by most of those around the world who are well positioned, the elite of most societies, as well as their intellectuals, and the ones who speak out on issues — pundits, artists, national leaders, celebrities, and such. It is mostly the silent majority who admires the American ideal, not those who rule over them.

In nearly every country around the globe, it is well understood that the kind of society that America had at one time aspired to become, a fully free society, would take seriously the contention that everyone is equal in having the unalienable natural — not government-granted — rights to life, liberty, and the pursuit of happiness, among others. And this means that no one may rule others without their consent.

Now consider how many countries around the globe are under the rule of some dictator or family or clergy or single political party! How can anyone imagine that in such societies those on top would eagerly welcome the notion that America was founded on? Sure, that notion is far from having been fully realized, even in the United States, although more so here than in most other places. And most folks in the United States do take seriously their right to their own lives, if not all their liberties and all the ways they might pursue happiness. Out of this has arisen a society in which few apologize for wanting to be happy, even for seeking a good deal of pleasure in life. And they take it as given that they need ask no one's permission to do this.

And there's the rub. In most other societies it is still pretty much accepted that people are not their own masters but subjects of someone else—the king, the government, or some other head of society. In many societies it is still usual to refer to the inhabitants as subjects, not citizens. So, how could the folks who enjoy the position of rulers, and those others who do well enough in such systems—the ones who can speak out in books, magazines, newspapers, and especially, political forums—admit that the American idea is a good one?

Add to this that elites and dreamers have always found fault with the bourgeoisie everywhere. Bourgeois values—which are mundane and not too dramatic, focused on having a decent life here on Earth, being successful in one's profession and so forth—offend those who aspire to the old-fashioned values of valor and glory and self-sacrifice, values found mostly in military battle! Nor does the bourgeoisie share the fantastic utopian notion of a perfect world in which all will be equally healthy, wealthy, and wise, made so by government regimentation!

America is the quintessential approximation to a bourgeois society, aspiring to be neither an aristocracy nor a utopian dreamland. In consequence, those around the globe who are sitting pretty, in societies that still carry on with the ancient regime of top-down rule, find America a threat and even go so far as to want to destroy it. And because of its relatively free institutions, sadly, a great many more Americans wallow in self-criticism than inflate themselves with pride. (Even I fall into that mode too often.)

It is interesting that many abroad who speak and write about the United States complain that Americans don't much care to hear them and pay little heed to their belly-aching. Well, no wonder! Why would most of the citizens and leaders of a country that has done better than most in pleasing the bulk of its ordinary citizens want to take advice from those who are basically flops at that mission? Why use even Western Europe as a model of how America should be governed, of which institutions it should cultivate and which it should dismantle?

No, America, though flawed and even losing sight of its virtues, is still a much better place for people who want to go about their own business—who don't want to be sacrificed to anyone else's dream, than any other place on earth. America has every right to dismiss most of what the finger-wagging leaders from abroad have to tell it. The default position should not be, "heed them for they have superior insight into public affairs," quite the contrary. More likely they could learn a thing or two from the new, but much to be admired, American experiment in social life.

The Trap of Humanitarian Wars

Irvine (California) Freedom News Wire, April 2003

In moral philosophy, altruism (or humanitarianism) has two versions. Under one, everyone must think of, and work for, others first, and what counts for this is up to the beneficiaries. In short, your help is what the beneficiaries consider to be help, not something objective one can know without knowing what the beneficiaries want. Under the other, one must still think of, and work for, others first, but what counts for this is something knowable by anyone, which could even conflict with what the beneficiaries would like to have done for them. The first is subjective, the second objective, altruism or humanitarianism.

In connection with domestic public policies, one can see this distinction clearly when government gives cash to welfare recipients, so they can get what they want for it, as opposed to when government gives them food or food stamps, insisting that the poor should get what is really good for them whether they like it or not. Both run risks — the first may amount to throwing money away since the poor may squander it; the second may offend by being paternalistic.

When a government goes to war for the sake of helping people in foreign countries, it is always a puzzle whether that government ought to follow the subjective or objective humanitarian policy. Should it just do for those who are in dire straits what they would like to have done for them, or should it provide what will actually do the people in these countries some good? The first approach trusts the people, rightly or wrongly, to know what will benefit them; the second trusts the invading forces to do so. This is a paradox of humanitarianism—to do good for others, we sometimes need to treat them as children and impose this good on them. Otherwise, all the help may be for nothing because those receiving it will squander it.

Many in Iraq, for example, seem happy to have gotten rid of Saddam Hussein's dictatorship, but this doesn't mean they want what the American leaders believe would be best for them, namely, a liberal democratic regime. Instead, huge rallies have been held to demand that Iraq become an Islamic country, run by Muslim clerics and other leaders. While Islamic rule may be more popular there than Saddam Hussein's rule was, it would be pretty harsh on the members of many minorities who do not embrace the Islamic faith, or not, at least, the version favored by the majority.

The impending democracy in Iraq would then mostly likely be illiberal. That is to say, those who do not share the faith of the majority would not have constitutional protection against being bullied by the majority. It would be as if, say, the Jehovah's Witnesses or some other evangelical faith became the majority in America and could impose its religious practices on everyone else. Instead, now the members of these sects must try to persuade people, and if sent on their way, they have to leave.

In fact, a just society would never tolerate having a morality or religion forcibly imposed, apart from the minimum protection of everyone's basic rights. That much protection is required so that everyone has the chance to choose whether to do this or that, including whether to embrace this or that faith. The rest is entirely a matter of choice, otherwise it doesn't count for much at all. Doing what is right or following a religion because of threats from others, especially government, doesn't count as doing what is right or following a religion at all.

Humanitarian or altruistic intervention is thus paradoxical. It aims to do good for others, especially political good, but then it treats these others as if they were children and can't be trusted with deciding how they should act. Yet, if a country's leaders have decided to tax their own people billions and billions to give real help to the people of other countries, and those people don't want this help but want to do what is politically wrong, how is one to proceed?

Perhaps the lesson to be gleaned here is that humanitarian wars are wrong, period. The billions of dollars the citizens of a country pay to keep a standing military should not be wasted on tasks that are hopeless. Americans should not be required to make the effort to help people who may not even want our help or only want it to do something not much better than that from which they were liberated.

It isn't as if Iraqis were incapable of taking part in a liberal democratic political order, but the large majority of them may not want to do so, even if that's wrong. American government officials should make up their minds — will they fight humanitarian wars that get them into the mess of having to impose the right system on unwilling people abroad, or will they confine themselves to fighting to defend the people they are supposed to serve?

If the second, then the only thing that made the war in Iraq just is that Saddam Hussein was very likely to unleash weapons of mass destruction against U.S. citizens and their allies. OK, so he cannot do this any longer. Thus now the U.S. military needs to leave and not play daddy or nanny to the Iraqis.

9. Endings

Berlin Wall
Came Down[*]

Back on November 9, 1989, I lived in Auburn, Alabama. On that morning I looked at the front page of my daily paper, and to my amazement, a cut-out map was shown on the front page with the name "Nickelsdorf" in big letters above a dot indicating a little town in Austria, about seven miles from the Hungarian border.

I was amazed because in 1953, in mid-October, I escaped from Hungary at that spot, leaving behind one-half of my family in order to meet the other half in the West. I was smuggled out of there by a professional, someone the American press would later deprecatingly call a "flesh peddler." I have never forgotten his good works!

The newspaper explained that the Hungarian government did something extraordinary. Some East Germans who came to Hungary wanted to visit their families in West Germany, and for the first time the Hungarian government permitted this, contrary to all expectations, allowing them to leave through Austria.

That was the beginning of the end of the Soviet Union's rule over Eastern Europe. It ended with the eventual demolition of that gross symbol of Soviet tyranny, the Berlin Wall.

The Iron Curtain, as it was dubbed by Winston Churchill, had turned out to be an embarrassment for Soviet socialism. It was a dividing line between what the Soviets had convinced themselves would be the haven of humanity, in contrast to the decrepit, decadent, and, yes, impoverished West that their leadership had been desperately denouncing for all sorts of reasons for over seventy years.

Soviet socialism was established because of Lenin's belief that one could hurry up history. Karl Marx, Lenin's philosophical teacher, had believed that after capitalism had run its course, socialism would emerge and, after that, communism would be reached as the final stage of humanity's development. All this was supposed to happen because of historical necessity, inevitably.

But there was a problem. Russia had never experienced capitalism, only bits and pieces of it here and there. So how could the Soviet Union be the leader of the march toward socialism, and after that, communism?

Marx gave a clue, in his preface to the Russian edition of the *Communist Manifesto*. He said that if the change to socialism in Russia were exported to other parts of the world—parts where capitalism had taken hold—then the impossible could be achieved, and Russia would become the next step toward communism.

Out of this came the efforts of the Soviet leaders to export their socialist system to all parts of the world, including much of Europe. Their first step was to make the Poles, Hungarians, East Germans, Rumanians, Czechs, Bulgarians, Albanians, and Yugoslavians all into dutiful socialists. The next step would then be to subvert the countries of Africa, Latin America, and even Western Europe. But to get this going the Eastern Europeans had to be cut off from Western Europe.

It is not clear whether the Soviet leaders realized early on that the Marxist story of humanity's progress toward communism was a ruse or whether most of them believed in it. In any case, they certainly saw in this story a way to secure for themselves the tyrannical powers that they had been wielding over millions of people for several decades, seven decades in the USSR and four decades in the rest of Europe.

In 1961 there was ample evidence that contact with the West would lead Eastern Europeans to lose any semblance of confidence in the Soviet myth of the march toward a prosperous communist society. That is when the Berlin Wall was built, as a way to keep East Germans from finding out how miserable their fate was. A lot of East Germans were fooled, but hundreds were not, many of them risking, and some losing, their lives in attempts to climb over the wall and seek refuge in the West.

Finally, once it became abundantly clear that Soviet socialism was a complete flop, no measure of credibility was left for the countries behind the Iron Curtain. And it was the Hungarian officials who seemed to have recognized this first. Mikhail Gorbachev, the last tyrant of the Evil Empire, contributed, of course, because in a desperate effort to revitalize the socialist experiment, he started glasnost, the policy of easing-up on government regimentation of the Soviet economy. As soon as he did this, he could kiss the socialist dream goodbye. Without the strong arm of government, socialism becomes a hopeless dream for anyone who has lived through some of it.

But it was the Hungarian government's policy of finally recognizing the insanity of keeping German families apart that precipitated the collapse of the Soviet empire. The Berlin Wall's demolition was the punctuation to that momentous decision.

Many in the West are upset that once the wall came tumbling down, the Soviet region didn't immediately become a haven of capitalist development and of other free institutions. This is like expecting a dysfunctional family to be able to recover immediately after a tragedy awakens its members to how badly they have been managing their lives.

The simple fact is that it will take several decades before the people of the former Soviet empire will recoup. They were injured in hundreds of different ways, and some of those who survived the ordeal have not even begun to get back on their feet.

Still, now, once the Soviet empire has decomposed, there is a chance for the people there to start living as free men and women, to organize their lives as they see fit, and perhaps even to prosper. To do all this, much needs to be accomplished — most important, a legal infrastructure must be set up that firmly establishes and protects the principles of private property rights and the integrity of contracts. Once that is achieved, the gradual rebuilding of the region can begin.

For now it is enough to simply celebrate ten years of life without the Soviet tyrants. In anyone's book that should be a promising beginning.

Post-Communist Traumas
East and West

Irvington-on-Hudson (New York) Freeman, May 1994

[We] cannot say that democratic institutions reflect a moral reality
and that tyrannical regimes do not reflect one, that tyrannies get
something wrong that democratic societies get right.
> Professor Richard Rorty, *New Republic,* July 1, 1991

During an international conference on political theory, several of us were sitting in a restaurant in Tallinn, Estonia.
Among us was a participant from Bucharest, Romania, a
young woman, who listened as some from the West poked
fun at the inefficiency of the Russians, who still have a significant presence in the Baltic countries and who happened
to be running this establishment. We noted the drabness
of the decor, the ineptness of the help, the slowness of the
service, and reminisced about the even worse olden days
when the gray-looking Russians who dominated the Communist culture ran roughshod over everyone in sight.

Suddenly we saw our friend from Bucharest in tears.
She apologized but was unable to keep herself from sob-
bing. We were stunned—we didn't know what we had done
to upset her. We all searched our minds for what we might
have said but could not come up with a sensible answer. In
a while, she calmed down a bit and told us.

All this amusing banter called to our friend's mind not
only what she had been living with all her life but what in
her country is still largely the case—the complete control of
a Soviet-style bureaucracy over society. She then went on

to recount, in halting English and tearfully, how the daily
lives of her family and friends had been trapped in the abyss
that so many in the West championed as the promising wave
of the future. She gave example after example of how people
had suffered, from moment to moment—how every ounce
of joy and pleasure, never mind genuine happiness, had
been rendered impossible and inconceivable for them. She
said that people simply lost the will to live, that they could
not even smile, not to mention laugh heartily, and that the
smallest matters, such as the way in which parents played
and talked with their children, had suffered from this totalitarian impact.

It is often only when one finds oneself facing the facts
directly, inescapably, that one can appreciate their meaning.
This is especially true about facts that so many people would
just as soon obscure with clever rationalizations.

In the West, especially in American newspapers, academic journals, and college classrooms, the Soviet empire
is nearly forgotten. People everywhere are talking about why
there isn't some major economic boom in response to this
fall. A *Business Week* editorial remarked, "Communism has
been vanquished in much of the globe, the victim of its own
failure to deliver a decent living to its citizens under its rule.
Yet capitalism in the industrialized nations is limping
along." It is as if "one, two, three," and our world will simply
put forty to seventy years of bloody dictatorship and command economy out of mind and bounce back as if nothing
had happened.

Assessing the Damage

The damage inflicted by the Communist reign is not nearly
well enough understood. It is certainly no longer treated as

a big deal. What has taken its place as a vital item of concern is just how bad conditions are in the wake of the efforts to live without communism, without the mighty Soviet state imposing its warped vision of human life on all the colonies within its sphere of impact. The question that seems to titillate the interest of many people is why the recovery is so slow, if it was needed in the first place. The question on the minds of many prominent journalists, for example, is: "What should be substituted for the admittedly harsh and clumsy form of socialism, in the wake of the evident unworkability of the freedoms that the people gained after the fall?"

Despite all the talk about free markets and free institutions in the newly liberated countries of Eastern Europe, the intellectual consensus among political theorists and scientists seems to be that some middle way is needed between socialism and capitalism. There is little encouragement for a truly vibrant capitalist system, either from our politicians and political theorists or from the voices of moral leadership.

Just consider what the word on this is from the Vatican secretary of state, Cardinal Angelo Sodano: "Capitalism is no less dangerous [than communism] because of its basic materialism and the unbridled consumerism and selfishness it encourages" (*La Stampa*, December 28, 1992). Rather than the truly productive capitalist system, the preferred choice seems to be social democracy, the welfare state, or communitarianism, a hybrid of liberalism and socialism, with the emphasis not on the value of the freedom of the individual, including freedom to engage in production and trade, but on the value of individuals' responsibilities to the community, not unlike the creed preached by Marx and his followers. The new vision involves a system in which free trade is here and there "permitted" but only under the watchful eyes of planners and regulators, who know just when to limit people's liberty good and hard.

The one system that gets the least play as the proper candidate to replace the tyranny just overthrown is free-market capitalism or, as the Europeans call it, classical liberalism. No, that would unleash all the beasts. Such freedom cannot work and must not be tried, lest anarchy and rapaciousness break out all over. Look what freedom's promise has already unleashed on Bosnia-Herzegovina. Look how greed and profiteering has already spread all over the old Soviet sphere. So the proper answer is not to let it happen — some people must become the stern tamers of the rest, if we could just quickly decide who is clever and dependable enough to take the reins of power.

Not only, then, is there little left of true capitalism and free-market economies in the West, but there is little chance of such a system taking over where Communist dictators failed. In addition to this, few people in the West seem to fully appreciate just how horrible the Soviet experiment really was and how difficult it is to recover from it. There are no expressions of earnest mea culpa anywhere. Publications such as the *Nation*, the *New Republic*, the *Progressive*, the *New York Times*, the *Washington Post*, and the hundreds of other more scholarly outlets or related media do not spend much time acknowledging that their different degrees of softness on communism, their thesis of the moral equivalency of capitalism and communism, and their subtle but evident apologies for the Lenins, Stalins, Brezhnevs, and others in the Soviet debacle may have had a bit to do with the horrors the people were subjected to and with their current difficulties in recovering from these horrors, starting a new life, and recapturing some measure of hopefulness and the will to live and flourish.

I was rereading *Naming Names* (New York: Viking, 1980), the book about the blacklist period in America during the 1950s by Victor Navasky, editor of the *Nation* (which is still proudly championing socialism with some kind of human face for all countries). In it Navasky made clear that he thought that despite the brutality of Soviet Marxism, there was something morally noble about the system because its intent was to help the poor and powerless. I also read some passages ridiculing the Russian-born American novelist Ayn Rand, who once claimed that a movie that depicted Russians smiling was a travesty, a sly propaganda piece, since no ordinary Russian could be presented in such a way without a gross distortion of the truth—it would be comparable to depicting Jews in concentration camps having a good time playing volleyball. Not that this may never have happened, but that highlighting such a scene in a work of fiction amounts to a vile distortion. Navasky and his ilk, of course, scoffed at this and still do.

A Complex, Painful Ordeal

But that is just what our Romanian friend was telling us about the millions and millions of victims of the Soviet terror, which only a lunatic could imagine to have been motivated by compassion and care. What is worse, today many of these same naïve reporters of the meaning and effect of Soviet socialism still do not appreciate just how complex and painful an ordeal it is to attempt to recover from it all.

People are not simply changing from one game to another when they finally are able to leave the Soviet system behind. They are undergoing recovery from extensive and prolonged injury to their whole being. They and everyone they knew and loved were beaten and derided and terrorized by thugs for decades on end. When they are finally left alone, they are expected to, as the song says, just pick themselves up, brush themselves off, and start all over again — with cheer in their hearts.

We are seeing some extremely painful recovery as well as relapses in the lives of those who were the victims of the Soviet experiment that so many of our comfortable intellectuals watched with vile neglect. We will see normal, imperfect human beings undergo a slow convalescence or stand around hesitatingly coping with new problems and nearly forgotten ones as well.

For the many people who have given their support to socialism and communism over the years — if only by not being brutally honest about them — on such grounds as that, well, these systems were motivated by compassion for the poor and downtrodden, the failure to see all this is blatant hypocrisy. The victims of the Soviet vision of human life deserve compassion and caring, and yet all they seem to be getting is a callous disregard for their plight and the quick judgment that they are, after all, unable to handle freedom, aren't they? What the yearning for self-justification will not permit some people to do in the face of the gravest of human tragedies!

Bulgarian Malaise

Orange County (California) Register, September 25, 1996

It was on August 25 that I tried to cross the border between Romania and Bulgaria, after I landed in Bucharest and took a cab to reach Ruse, the nearby Bulgarian border town, to meet a friend there. I had planned to rent a car. I had been assured by fax that I could take the rental car across the border, but when I landed at the airport, this proved to be false. So I took a cab, with a driver who spoke a bit of English and was confident he could get me to Ruse without any problems.

After a forty-five-minute drive, we came to the border. I was completely unprepared, on a Sunday afternoon, for the incredibly long line of vehicles that awaited us. I had asked my cabby, but he assured me there'd be no wait on a Sunday. The cars, trucks, buses, and every other kind of road transport one could imagine lined up to form a standing caravan of about seventy-five vehicles, with the people standing around or sitting on top of them, biding their time, without any apparent progress made in crossing the border, over the Danube on Friendship Bridge into Bulgaria.

The most conspicuous element of the scene was the constant milling about of shirtsleeved officials, collecting bribes for (mostly false) promises to let a vehicle move up a bit, to get in front of the one ahead. My cabby told me repeatedly that I needed to pay, that without bribing several of these officials in their blue shirts we would never get ahead. I, in turn, had the impression that if I paid one bribe,

I would be sunk—they would then be able to do with me whatever they wanted, since I had committed a crime and would be forever vulnerable to being manipulated. So I resisted.

After twenty minutes of getting a feel for the situation, I decided to get out of the car, walk to the front of the line, and do something, whatever, to try to move on. In the little wooden building, I saw, through a window, one uniformed man checking through countless passports, with seven others standing outside biding their time, chain-smoking, while the crowd waited patiently for something to happen.

I approached one of the idle officers and implored him to let me cross right then. He took my passport and disappeared into the building, only to emerge in ten minutes followed by a stocky officer with my passport in hand. By this time, my cabby had managed to buck the line and reach me, and I was soon back sitting in the cab next to him. The stocky official looked into the driver-side window and shook his head. "Impossible," he said, "you cannot cross the border now. It is impossible." He went on in this vein for another five minutes or so. And then, giving me back my passport, he waved us on across the now-raised barrier.

We hightailed it toward Bulgaria. But I couldn't resist looking back, checking to see if some kind of mass protest had erupted in the wake of what had just happened.

There was no movement. The hundreds of drivers and passengers were just standing around, eating sandwiches, drinking sodas, chatting, laughing, paying no heed to the tall, gray-haired foreigner who had bullied himself across a border they had been waiting for three hours, and would continue to wait for another two or four hours, to cross. It was just life as they knew it—it all depended on the caprice of the border guards in whose hands their fate lay.

This episode was followed by repeated examples of people showing complete subservience to official ineptitude and inefficiency. At railway stations no information was forthcoming from those charged with the responsibility of providing it—instead, these officials would look at those who sought their help with annoyance and just shake their heads to indicate that no information was forthcoming, not just then. The attitude was clear: "There is nothing in it for me if I help you; I can decide whether I will or not, whatever my official position may seem to promise." But no one protested—I was alone in showing any resistance to such widespread official phlegmatism.

Bureaucrats in Bulgaria seem to see themselves as autocrats, not as professionals with some kind of responsibility to serve the public. Even after six years of post-Communist life, the country is still suffocating from the attitudes people learned during forty years of socialist regimentation. There is no sign of "the customer is king," far from it. And no one seems to demand it, either. Even private shops are filled with employees who seem to look on themselves as doing customers a favor by selling them bread, butter, postcards, or dinner.

With only a few exceptions—involving rare folks who have managed to rescue their spirits from the morass of apathy and hopelessness—the country is filled with people who do not want to fight for anything, who do not expect their lives to be improved by making any effort to do so. Their fate, they seem to think, is sealed.

Socialism kills more than economic growth—indeed, the reason it kills that and a lot more is that it destroys the souls of citizens. From such destruction it will take a good while to recover.

U.S. Congress v. the INS: In the Matter of Elian Gonzales*

This case has gotten me somewhat riled up because when I was fourteen, I was smuggled out of Communist Hungary illegally. My mother, who lived in Hungary with her husband and two daughters, both ten years my junior, was in on the plans, but later she had to pretend not to have known anything about it, otherwise she would have been put in prison.

Once I reached Vienna safely, I wrote her a postcard apologizing for running away from home so that she could have some "evidence" to show the government goons hounding her that she had had nothing to do with my escape. Still, for ten years or more after that, once or twice a year the police would call her downtown to question her about my successful escape. She had to deny knowing anything about it and pretend to want me back. When suddenly the hounding stopped, she concluded that the person who had her file had probably died or retired.

Now, no one such case is exactly like another—these are exactly the kind of cases used to test rules, laws, moral principles, and so forth. They are exceptional, and no easy, straightforward solution to them is possible. Which is why it is curious that the Clinton administration refuses to approve of a court settlement in which precedent, pertinent testimony, rules of evidence, and the rest would get a close hearing before judgment is made, and the boy's fate decided.

In several media forums there have been interesting exchanges between Republicans and Democrats, both of whom disavow any intention to politicize the case. But in fact New York's Democratic congressman Charlie Rangle flatly and unhesitatingly supported the Clinton-Reno-INS decision to send back Elian. The Republicans I have heard, in contrast, have been advancing several arguments that, put together, make a good case not so much for keeping the boy here as for leaving the decision about him to be reached by a court of law.

Now when there are serious disputes about rights in a free society, this is where government is supposed to have a role, not in banning drugs, saving forests, or putting up monuments. Dispute resolution is unique because although sometimes the parties commit themselves ahead of time to abide by what an arbitration board decides, often only force brings them to the same table. The fact that rights seem to have been violated makes such force justified when ordinarily it would not be. This kind of legal force is supposed to be used with extreme care—due process—so that everyone's rights are closely guarded, and the most impartial, rational decision is reached.

This is in contrast to a bureaucratic decision, made by highly partisan agency heads, who usually follow party interests. They are often committed to serving special purposes, even as they insistently proclaim that they are serving the public interest. That is the nature of the welfare state and of nearly all institutions associated with it, so what Clinton, Janet Reno, and the INS are doing here is nothing unusual.

Because of the adversarial system of jurisprudence, the

courts are likely to be more fair and just. Each side gets to
air its case, which will not happen if the decision is left to
some department of a politicized government administration. But Reno and her crew at the Department of Justice
(DOJ) and the INS sing the tune of their boss, Bill Clinton.
That is natural.

Clinton has a history of pragmatism about ideals, but
where he does embrace them, they lean toward the Left. He
has little serious commitment to values but does favor the
worldview of those who sympathize with Fidel Castro's
efforts to make an egalitarian country out of Cuba. As to the
rest, whatever works for extending his power and, now, his
wife's, is the usual motivating principle at the Clinton White
House.

As to the future of six-year-old Elian Gonzales—
whether Communist Cuba is where he should be sent to
grow up or whether he should be allowed to stay in the
United States (where clearly his mother and probably even
his father want him to live)—that is of no great consequence
to Mr. Clinton. Why should it be? How can such considerations get him what he is after, political influence, especially
with the more outspoken ideologues in his liberal Democratic political culture (including Al Gore)?

While Republicans—who also have their knee-jerk
responses to public affairs—might be expected to just want
to sock it to Fidel Castro, it looks to me as if their position
is more measured, level-headed, and consistent with the
judicial philosophy of a free society. They have proposed
that the case be subjected to a careful, thorough investigation under the scrutiny of judges and opposing attorneys,
witnesses, and so on, and will go with whatever the result.
That is how a tough choice needs to be made, not by having
partisan bureaucrats decide from high above.

An Old Moral Blindness
Revisited*

The flap about awarding Elia Kazan a special Academy Award last Sunday raises some issues that should not be forgotten. Kazan is a Hollywood ex-Communist who testified before the House Unamerican Activities Committee (HUAC) hearings when that congressional body was making ill-conceived efforts to counter the influence of communism in American culture. He named names.

No one can, I believe, offer a good defense of the HUAC and its efforts. It is the quintessential feature of a free society that people do not get punished for what they believe, however awful their beliefs are. (This, by the way, is something that many who condemned the HUAC's actions in the 1950s are finding unobjectionable now, when hate crimes have become a target of left-wing legislation! If Communists — who, after all, supported Stalinist Soviet Russia and advocated the overthrow of the U.S. government — ought not be hounded for what they believe and feel, neither should racists and others who hate with a fierce passion.) Unless there is clear evidence that someone or some group is embarking on violence against others, including members of the government, no official counteractions should be taken.

Yet, just as with those who seek to punish hatred — by making a hate crime something more heinous than an ordinary crime — those who wanted to punish Communists and their sympathizers can be viewed with some measure of appreciation for their eagerness. Communists, after all, supported a regime and its worldwide imperialist efforts, which were just as bad, if not worse, than the Nazis'. They deserve no praise for their "integrity," any more than a Nazi or a member of the KKK does. Communists were out-and-out enemies of the American way of life of individualism, free enterprise, private property rights, and the rest.

But there are those who disagree. Among them Victor Navasky is perhaps most prominent, the author of *Naming Names*, a book that discussed with great moral indignation the alleged evils of turning in Communists and fellow travelers. Navasky is also the editor of the *Nation*, the most openly left-wing and widely read weekly magazine in this country.

Navasky has argued that one reason turning against Communists is bad, while turning against Nazis is good, is that Communists were inspired by moral ideals. Among these is the improvement of the working class, helping the poor, rejecting the economic class system, and so on. He admits—rather perfunctorily, for my money—that the Soviet Communists used evil methods to try to achieve these admirable goals, but he urges us to judge Communists and ex-Communists in America and elsewhere by these goals, not the methods they were often duped into supporting.

Navasky went around before the Oscars condemning Kazan, as did a bunch of ex-Communist directors and writers who had lost career opportunities after being identified as Communists or ex-Communists. But his attempt to exonerate these folks just will not wash.

To start with, one can associate every vicious movement with some decent objectives. The Nazis, for example, championed clean and healthful living and the upgrading of the human species, as many people do who are enamored with health, athletics, sports, nutrition, and so forth. Even the Communists want to bring about a human race that is free of foibles and bad habits. There is really no difference between the two ideologies at all. And they share each other's unabashed use of the most vicious means for achieving their goals. One size fits all is their motto, and they are willing to shove it down everyone's throat.

The "ratting" done by Elia Kazan was no different from someone ratting on others who commit robbery, murder, rape or on those who want to cover up such crimes and aid and abet their perpetrators. Today's advocates of making hate a crime are plenty happy when they find some skinhead or ex-militia member turn against an old buddy, because if the activity is vicious enough, turning those in who engage in it is something commendable.

Elia Kazan's mistake was only to have accepted the legitimacy of our federal government's technique for trying to combat communism. He did nothing wrong when he named names. Nor do those who turn in Mafia operatives do anything wrong. Indeed, that is often the only decent thing they can do after having cooperated with the organization's criminal conduct.

So the issue really isn't about being a snitch. We should like anyone who snitches against folks who are hurting others. It is only when we consider the activities innocent or harmless that turning someone in is the wrong kind of ratting. A police informant who lets us know about a robber or murderer is a good guy. One who turns in prostitutes or junkies is a bad guy.

Kazan wasn't informing on a bunch of innocent, persecuted people but on supporters of Stalin who, like Hitler, was a mass murderer. To show all this sympathy for those in Hollywood who gave aid and comfort to Stalin betrays a warped sense of political values.

Elia Kazan was right not to have acquiesced to calls that he should apologize. It is he who is owed an apology for having been vilified for a minor transgression while trying to ferret out some of the really bad blood in Hollywood.

Glasnost in Chile?

Chronicles of Culture (Rockford, Illinois), August 1989

Pinochet is getting no credit for it. Yet at the same time, General Secretary (and now also President) Gorbachev's policies are being hailed as major breakthroughs, departures from the previous (Brezhnev) era. These policies are ·thought to hold out great promise for the people of the Soviet Union if they can only succeed. Glasnost (openness) and perestroika (reconstruction) are widely praised by commentators as important moves to advance the Soviet Union toward a better society. There are some skeptics, of course — David Slater (in the *New Republic*) doubts that glasnost can work. But on the whole, writers in the *Nation*, the *New Yorker*, and other prominent publications express basic respect for Mikhail Gorbachev's intentions and efforts.

In contrast, there is no one who likes General Pinochet. The question is, why? While he has been a ruthless opponent of political freedom in Chile for almost as long as he has been in power, in 1980 he helped forge a new constitution for that country that paves the way to full-scale political democracy. We have just witnessed one result of this constitutional reform — an election in Chile to decide whether Pinochet may serve for another full term or whether he has to step down within a year after his term expires. It looks like the general intends to abide by the outcome, and in March 1990 elections will be held to decide who will govern Chile. Pinochet has also established an economy in Chile that has led to greater prosperity there than in any other Central and Latin American country. While Chile has pockets of poverty, the country nevertheless has had lower inflation and higher employment than its neighbors.

We do not know what Pinochet will or will not do. He is still in power, and the constitution that gives him that power is far from expressing the will of even the majority of the people, much less protecting the rights of a minority.

What do we know about Gorbachev? He has proposed no change to the Soviet constitution, a document that explicitly prohibits anyone in the Soviet Union from criticizing the Soviet government. The law may not always be enforced, but it is crucial that there is no legal obstacle to invoking it. Has Gorbachev advocated changing the nature of Soviet society? No; he simply regards some earlier policies as following from "distortions of socialism." He has no desire, judging by his own words, to abandon Lenin's "genuine socialism." The means of production in the Soviet Union will continue to be collectively owned and thus exposed to government regimentation. Perestroika may lead the state to relax its regime, but not to abdicate its role as ultimate sovereign. If one recalls that in Marxist socialist theory the primary means of production is human labor, Gorbachev is unambiguously committed to treating Soviet citizens as mere cells in the body of the state. Nor should we lose sight of the fact that Gorbachev was an enthusiastic follower of Brezhnev. His role in the KGB cannot be ignored either.

Of course, Pinochet's partial embracing of capitalism — through his University of Chicago–trained finance minister Herman Buchi, who has recently resigned — does not mean that Chile enjoys a free marketplace, in which everyone's private property rights are fully acknowledged and respected. Yet at least Pinochet seems to be bent on heading toward that kind of system, one that makes the individual sovereign, not the state.

Why then are American intellectuals so contemptuous of Pinochet but not critical (indeed they are quite welcoming) of Gorbachev? Why would Gore Vidal, for example, praise the Soviet leader so highly—calling one of his speeches the most profound political talk he has ever encountered? (And Vidal is the author of the novel *Lincoln*!) Is it that for most American intellectuals there are no enemies to the left?

Hungary 1990: A Visit to an Abandoned Homeland

Orange County (California) Register, September 30, 1990

In October of 1953 I was smuggled out of Hungary by a professional "flesh peddler," as *Time* magazine referred to them in a 1980 story. I was fourteen years old. Stalin had died in March, and the country was a dreary place, with little hope that the Soviet Union's reign would ever end.

Since that time I have become a nearly full-fledged American—I served in the Air Force, completed study for three degrees (all in philosophy), and made myself a family man as well. I worked hard to shed my connections to the old country, so much so that on the rare occasions when I bumped into other émigré Hungarians, they resented the fact that I spoke fluent English with only the slightest accent and that my Hungarian was rather inept.

Now and then, I ran into Hungarian scholars at international conferences, and I was, therefore, aware of the gradual changes in Hungary's political and cultural climate. Yet it still came as something of a shock that in 1989 Hungary broke with orthodox Soviet hegemonic policy and opened its borders so that East German visitors could escape in droves from the Eastern bloc. When I picked up the newspaper in my driveway one day and saw the map of the Hungarian border regions near Nickelsdorf, Austria, the very same place where my own escape took place almost exactly thirty-five years before, I knew that things were going to be changing much faster than I had dared to hope, let alone predict.

I don't wish to dwell on the politics of the changes taking place in what used to be the Soviet-bloc countries—that subject is on everyone's mind and fills the pages of magazines, journals, newspapers, and other publications these days. Instead I want to reflect on what it is to experience being given a chance to recover something, one's home roots, including feelings, memories of sights, sounds, images, tastes, and the more subtle features of an atmosphere one has tried so hard to erase from one's brain.

During the last thirty years, I have worked hard on not being tied to my homeland. I felt that it was useless to keep up empty hopes, to dwell on lost chances. I was going to be very positive about my acquisition of a new home. I wanted to become an American—I had read American novels when I was young, and their atmosphere contrasted so starkly with what I had experienced that if the opportunity presented itself, I would jump this ship and board that other, one that seemed clearly to my liking.

Indeed, I went about for much of my life making it clear to myself, through my work as a political philosopher, why leaving Communist Hungary and becoming an American citizen had such attraction for me. Was it merely a personal prejudice? Was I a born bourgeois? Was I elevating an accidental fact of my life into something mythically significant? I had written and edited books—*Human Rights and Human Liberties* (Chicago: Nelson-Hall, 1975) and *The Main Debate: Communism versus Capitalism* (New York: Random House, 1987)—dealing with such issues.

Suddenly, the main reason I had decided to change homelands was evaporating—Hungary seemed to be free again, or getting there slowly. What should I do? I still had the chance to reconsider, to reexamine, to see if somehow, despite my reasonably successful acclimation to the United States of America, I would not find Hungary much more of a home.

In the spring of 1990, I was invited to lecture in Hungary on political philosophy. The audience would be international, mostly composed of university students from countries previously under Soviet control. I would be able to lecture in English, the official language of the seminars. It fit in my schedule. So I accepted.

In August 1990, I went to Szirak, to the renovated castle there, and spent a week giving lectures and taking in the experience of being back in Hungary. I visited Budapest, one of the world's most attractively laid-out cities, and I met with Hungarian scholars of impeccable (classical) liberal credentials. I was even invited to spend a term teaching in the country. My daughter, Kate, came with me and was shown, by relatives, all the places of my early youth—apartments where I lived, schools I attended, my grandmother's residence, and so on.

It was all a bit too fast for me, I admit. I cannot even say that my thoughts are fully collected now. But my impressions are clear enough.

Hungary, not unlike other countries under Soviet oppression for the last forty years or so, is now emerging from a period of colonial occupation. It is by no means near recovery—the diagnosis of what ails it hasn't even begun. While there is a large influx of Western European tourism and commerce, there is also uncertainty about whether the people of this country can cope with the challenges a relatively free society poses for people. The economy is likely to be transformed into a relatively free market, judging by how well the intellectual community is receiving the advice of Janos Kornai in his book *The Road to a Free Market* (New York: W.W. Norton, 1990). Kornai is professor of economics at both Harvard University and the University of Budapest and has been a student of socialist economies from the mid-1950s. He advises radical reform, not dilly-dallying at all.

Can a country accustomed to the mirages of a static economy such as socialism ready itself for a dynamic market system? And how will people be able to cope with the knowledge that thousands of officials who inflicted the damage to their country will probably retire contentedly to Lake Balaton, experiencing no adverse consequences from their criminal complicity? How will people be able to suffer the fallout of forty years of mismanagement when they know that the culprits are treated with kid gloves, mostly because there would be no great advantage to anyone from meting out the demands of justice?

I was noticing in the eyes of every intelligent Eastern European a sense of fearful anticipation, a plea for prudence on the part of all, a hope for a patient and successful convalescence. Hungary, like most of the other countries in question, will not only have to cope with the damage done to it by socialism and communism. It will also have to cope with leftover problems, unresolved social, cultural, and religious difficulties that are resurfacing everywhere.

A free society is no guarantee of universal happiness—only of the opportunity to strive for such happiness. Tyranny suppresses not only what is good in society but also some of what ails it. And with the reemergence of liberty, all of this will surface again.

I can only wish that the people of Hungary have the will, intelligence, and virtue to remake their country into a thriving culture and not allow it to be crushed by all the adversities that face it. But I know that I am an American, with

my roots in Hungary, my life in America. My adopted homeland has its own troubles, and I have returned to cope with
my share of them. I may go to Hungary for visits, even for
professional excursions, but I will always return home to
America, where my life must be lived as well as possible. I
am fortunate, however, that I had the chance to make sure
that this was what I wanted to do and that this chance was
made possible by the emergence of my original country
from a very dark period, one that I can only hope will never
be repeated.

A Most Peculiar
Nostalgia

Orange County (California) Register, November 25, 2002

Imagine yourself on a plane browsing through the *SkyMall* magazine catalog, finding a nice old U-boat clock shown, with a swastika displayed on it prominently, offered at the reasonable price of $80.00. Or how about a nice hat that proudly carries on its front the Iron Cross of the Third Reich, for a modest $150 or, if made of fine fur, for $450? I am not certain, but I doubt *SkyMall*'s management would be hailed for its sensitivity—a little like illustrating its pages with little Sambo figures from the deep south, isn't it?

Now think of yourself as a refugee from some Soviet-bloc country, as I am and as are millions of Americans, who runs across the clock from a Soviet submarine in *SkyMall* magazine, and a mouton and mink ushankas, promoted as memorabilia from the worst tyranny in human history, offered for us all to wear in good spirits. A bit crass?

But that isn't all. What if National Public Radio offered up some of the wonderful performances of Beethoven or Brahms from, well, the National Socialist Symphony Orchestra of the Third Reich, for its listeners to enjoy performances of great music from the past? Or what if some film festival on, say, a classic movie cable channel were to feature, without comment and as simple film art, the works of some German director who just did what she was told but did it beautifully?

Many of us know well that nothing like that could happen. The Nazis had no redeeming social value to offer up, period, and quite understandably so. Their regime was so vile, so horrible, so inhumane that any thought of enjoying some part of it, even if in principle distinguishable from what the Nazis as Nazis did, is itself nearly unbearable.

Yet here we are. In thousands of airline backseat pockets around America, people are able to find catalogues advertising memorabilia from the Soviet era, and hundreds of university radio stations, getting their programming from NPR, present to all their loyal, elite listeners classical tunes from the various orchestras of the USSR. What is the not-so-hidden message here, anyway?

Well, for my money, it is that a great many of those people who call the shots for what counts as palatable in recent human history seem to believe that while the Nazis were a categorically nasty lot — never mind that they may have made some movies and played some classical music well enough — the butchers of the Soviet era don't qualify for such total dismissal. And why is this? Because for most of these folks who tell us what counts as culturally palatable, the Soviet era was merely a somewhat rough experiment, a good thing that sadly didn't quite work out.

Stalin, and Lenin before him — and the others who followed, and all their lackeys, all those little helpers of history who carried out the murder of roughly 20 million innocent human beings in the period of about fifty years, with a good deal of moral support from the intellectual and cultural elite of the rest of the globe — were, well, just misguided, off a bit, nothing to get all excited about. In contrast, Hitler and his gang — who were not embarking on launching the international socialist revolution but merely a national socialist program, although they murdered about 6 million Jews and gypsies and homosexuals and others — were clearly, unambiguously, and definitely a contemptible lot. They were not aiming for the liberation of the workers of the world as they perpetrated their mass murder, their genocide, so they cannot be embraced in any shape or form. The Soviets, however—well, at any rate, some of them—meant well. And isn't it that thought that counts? It's a crock, of course—the Nazis had some good enough goals, like preserving high culture, reinvigorating Germany, and molding the people into model human beings, a goal shared by many respectable people in history who, however, wouldn't go about getting there on the path the Nazis tried. Both, the Soviets and the Nazis, had some ideals, more or less worthy, but employed means that left those ideals pretty much in total disgrace.

At a recent conference honoring the memory of the philosopher Sidney Hook, a man of the anticommunist Left— a democratic socialist who actually saw Karl Marx as someone who would have been horrified at what the Soviets made of his thought—some erudite folks made no bones about seeing things roughly along those old lines. While, yes, Stalin was a terribly vicious excuse for a human being, to get obsessed with anticommunism, as they thought Hook had been in the latter part of his life, was rather uncouth, not worthy of a serious person. Anyone like Hook, who didn't take Joseph McCarthy and McCarthyism to be the worst thing America has seen in its recent political history, comparable to nothing less than slavery itself, but who thought that McCarthy, though a nuisance, was still relatively small-fry compared to Stalin and his supporters, well, such a person just didn't cut it in the eyes of these politically correct people.

They just will not learn. Maybe their early blindness to just how vicious, how vile the Soviets were makes it difficult for these folks to own up to their misjudgments even now.

The consequence of it may, however, be more serious than lots of folks think: it may encourage a perpetuation of the idea that the Soviet horrors were not much to fret about and that remembering those who stood by the side of these butchers is sort of cute, even nostalgic.

10. Life Is Good

A Fan of KLON-FM (Now KKJZ), 88.1

Orange County (California) Register, May 18, 2002

It is customary for pundits to bellyache about the world. If you were to put together all the writings of columnists, you would think there is no joy at all in our lives. Indeed, just the other day I had to defend the view that, no, I do not think our culture is bankrupt; I just believe our political system could use a lot of mending.

True, there is the problem — notice, another one! — that folks do not express their joy or delight much, not at least in public forums. Instead it is their dismay, complaints, annoyances, fears, and so on that get broadcast. CNN-TV is, as I once called it, the Crisis News Network TV, and hardly any good news ever gets on the air there, though now and then one may find some amusing stories stuck at the end of the thirty minutes of headlines.

A while back, however, I was reminded of how misguided it is to constantly complain. It was in the form of a bumper sticker I saw on a car in Atlanta, Georgia, on my way to the airport. It was sponsored by the Seventh-Day Adventists, and it read: "Notice the good and praise it."

Well, today I have simply wanted to spend some of my "ink" to praise a part of the culture I have enjoyed ever since I moved out to Orange County, California, in January 1997. Actually, I knew of its pleasures even before that, since every time I landed at Los Angeles Airport, I immediately set my rental car's radio to it.

What I want to do is congratulate the on-air and off-air staff of KLON-FM radio, the California State University Long Beach jazz and blues station, for its wonderful array of personalities and, especially, musical offerings. I do not remember the names of all of them. I am one who has to talk to folks and see their names in print before I remember them. But I do know that there is a Helen, a Chuck, a Gary Wagman, all of whom, together with their colleagues, achieve a unique atmosphere for their listeners. I venture to speculate that Helen's infectious laughter-holler has become a spiritual aid to many listeners!

Of course, in the end it is the incredible material this group is able to work with that makes their offering so fabulous. If you are not a fan of jazz and blues, this will not resonate with you, although if you like a bit of the most essentially American performance art, you will at least be glad to know that KLON is the number-one jazz station in the country.

I have dreamt for a long time of having a radio station near me that I can listen to all the time, at home, in my car, even in the background at my office—carrying the kind of music that never bores and indeed often sends me. KLON's repertoire finally fulfills that hope. Add to that the sparkling personalities, young or old, and you have a small part of your life on a winning course, that's for sure.

Now and then, this is almost a liability since I just must listen Saturdays and Sundays, between 2 and 7, to "Nothing but the Blues" with Gary the Wagman. And I just have to catch the next Diana Krall rendition of "If I had You" or Shirley Horn's "But Beautiful." Even worse, I quite often have to go out and buy a CD from which a song simply enchanted me. Because of the litigious atmosphere in which we live, I fear that my three kids will soon be suing KLON for inducing me to "squander" on jazz and blues CDs the small inheritance they are looking forward to! My planned defense: This is all in the way of a significant contribution to the finest part of American culture. I am buying the music to advance the public interest, of course. Sure!

When I was an undergraduate at Claremont Men's College, back in the early 1960s, I had an hour-long radio program on Sundays during which I played nothing but Erroll Garner renditions of wonderful classic American melodies from the works of Gershwin, Kern, Porter, Berlin, and others. I was terrible, despite the fantastic, bouncing music of that late great piano player, so I quit and decided to earn degrees in philosophy instead of becoming a DJ. A very good decision, considering all the talent we come across on KLON and how I could never have competed with that.

Sure, there is other wonderful stuff on the radio, and I do listen now and then to the University of Southern California classical station and sometimes to classic rock. (I have finally, after years of masochism, given up on the NPR stations because they are, I have discovered, bad for my nerves.) But I do not think anything quite matches what KLON has to offer me, and I wanted simply to make note of this, following the advice of that bumper sticker from the Seventh-Day Adventists, "Notice the good and praise it!" Even if it is just a little thing, a personal one.

Sinatra's Pizzazz

Orange County (California) Register, May 19, 1998

In 1955 I was a teen whose father wanted to make him into a champion crewman. My father had won the European pair-oar without coxswain (that is, a third person steering the boat) in 1936, but he never got to race in the Olympics because that event was canceled due to war!

So when I was finally smuggled out of Hungary, my father began putting into effect his plan to make me a rowing champion. Only I had no inclination to comply. So there were some very unpleasant scenes in our house, mostly his beating me because he didn't like that my plans didn't always include his.

By this time I was enamored of American pop culture, mostly encountered through the radio broadcasts of the Armed Forces Network. I listened eagerly to all the American pop artists, including, of course, Frank Sinatra. My father's favorite was, in contrast, the more mild-mannered and conventional Bing Crosby, someone I liked but not as much as Sinatra.

One day Sinatra's "Learning the Blues" came on the radio while the family was sitting around the house, and my father noticed that I was snapping my fingers to the tune. He was furious and began to deride both me and Sinatra, good and hard. I was forbidden, from then on, from listening to anything Sinatra sang. Whenever my father was out of the house and returned, he would check the radio to see if it was warm, to make sure I didn't sneak and listen behind his back.

Over the years I always wondered why he showed such hostility to a mere pop idol. And I believe I have the answer, finally.

Frank Sinatra was the pop-artist embodiment of cockiness, brashness, defiance. "I Did It My Way" became his signature tune once he got older, and rightly so. Not that he did it his way all the time, I am pretty sure—no one can bring that off in a complicated world (with agents, producers, a demanding public, and a government that likes to remind everyone who has the police on its side). But in spirit Ol' Blue Eyes projected nothing less than rebellion, the "in your face, you who want to push me around" attitude. His tone, the choice of his songs, all spoke the message: let me be free to do my thing!

I have no illusions that Frank Sinatra was a great political sage. Nor does it matter—not everything in life has to have political merit. Being a wonderful entertainer over nearly a lifetime is plenty of achievement for anyone. Sinatra joins such greats as Fred Astaire, Jack Benny, and the rest, in this role.

But there is something about certain American entertainers that one will never find in other cultures—I realized this when I reflected on the appeal of stars such as Robert Mitchum and even James Garner. There is a relaxed, casual self-confidence they project, saying through their performances: "A human being can do it, do it right, and need not be too taken with himself while he does it."

As I reflected on Sinatra's legacy of projecting this attitude, I wondered if this element in American culture wasn't fading away? Is this culture, perhaps, becoming like all the others, a class-ridden, stodgy place where good manners, deference, and other forms of self-suppression are valued over the assertiveness that America has been admired for, especially by the ordinary people around the world?

How I Learned to
Love the Rich

Orange County (California) Register, July 11, 1993

I came to America as a rather poor immigrant and, after leaving home at age eighteen, became dirt poor. But I have also been fortunate and industrious enough not to end up on welfare.

Not that everything went smoothly, but all in all, I got nearly everything I set out to gain, including a superb education, a career that many people could envy, wonderful children, a great deal of travel, some of the best friends one could ask for, and at least a tolerable economic life that sustains me well enough, although by no means in luxury.

There clearly are many people who are far more prosperous than I am. And I could easily benefit from having a good deal more money.

Yet, I have never known envy in my life. Somehow the sight of others with greater wealth has never led me to desire to exchange my life for theirs. Nor, especially, have I ever felt ill will toward those who are rich. And there are some good reasons for my pleasure with them, even if I can hardly think of myself in their shoes.

For one, the rich remind me that if I wanted to aspire to be one of them, I would have a decent chance at it. Some rich people started nearly as low on the economic ladder as I did. But they wanted to be well off and found a way to do this. I know some people who are millionaires, a few who probably have a billion or so, and because I know them, I can see that the way movies or sitcoms or pulp novels depict the rich is hopelessly inaccurate. None of these folks is mean or greedy or amoral. Quite the opposite.

Another reason I welcome the existence of the rich in our society is that without them we and millions of others would scarcely have a chance at the occasional luxury, a taste of the finer aspects of dining, entertainment, decoration, art, and culture in general.

Who but the rich sustain good restaurants? Who but the rich make possible fine porcelain or jazz clubs or beautiful rugs or fancy furniture, not to mention stunning architecture and enthralling theater? I cannot afford to support artists, musicians, actors, great chefs, and the other people who create and produce some of the marvelous features of our culture, nor can my friends with middle or low incomes.

But once in a blue moon we all manage to go to a great French restaurant, an art gallery, a neighborhood where fashionable estates are located, or a shopping center that features exquisite merchandise. I and those like me would not be able to support elegant ocean cruisers, delightful automobiles, or great sports events such as Wimbledon or the America's Cup. But there are those who can and I, for one, am extremely glad for that.

This is one of the reasons — although not the main one — for my distress about the rich-bashing that is so common in our culture. I find it disgusting how the envious among us would rather destroy the rich than witness the gap between their modest wealth and the great wealth of the rich.

I find it especially loathsome that so many American politicians, who ought to know better, gladly capitalize on this envy and persist in using the rich as a scapegoat for their own unwillingness to do the right thing, namely, concentrate on defending us from foreign and domestic aggressors and leave us be, to fend for ourselves in peace, however much economic disparity this may generate (far less, incidentally, than is generated in societies where politicians try to even things out and run the entire country's economy into the ground).

Of course, the first thing to be said about the rich is that they have every right to seek their kind of life, so long as they do this in peace. But there is also this point, namely, that their existence is of enormous benefit to the rest of us, not just in creating jobs and increasing national wealth but in keeping culture at a level that is there for all of us to enjoy, to save up for once in a while, even if we do not wish to live the intense life they are willing to live.

Now Beauty
Is a Liability?

Irvington-on-Hudson (New York) Freeman, January 1992

Back in 1974 I started editing an interdisciplinary scholarly journal, focused mainly on social and political issues. After the journal got some attention among colleagues in different fields—mostly in my field of philosophy—we began to receive submissions from scholars of a wide array of persuasions.

I recently was reminded of one such submission, which we turned down after it had gone through the regular peer-review process. What reminded me was a book review in the *New York Times* of a work in which the author, herself a beautiful woman, discussed how awful it is that men have imposed high standards of good looks on women throughout the ages.

The paper argued that it is morally wrong, indeed unjust, to heed the appearance of a person when one considers asking him or her out for a date. Why is that so, one might ask? The reason is that a person's natural good looks are not something he or she earned and thus shouldn't benefit from. Only if one chooses a date or even a friend because of something good that the person has done of his or her own free will does it qualify as a morally proper act.

Now at first blush there is a ring of plausibility to all this. If one is considering rewarding people for something, surely it is important to choose what they have achieved as grounds for the prize. Olympic medals aren't given for just being tall or healthy. The Nobel prize isn't handed out just for having a high IQ. A person has to accomplish something to deserve accolades. Only on television do folks regularly get prizes as a matter of pure luck.

But when I choose a companion or date, am I handing out rewards? It's quite self-deluded to look at it that way. Rather, one is choosing a benefit for oneself. One wants the company of someone who is pleasant, appealing, and the like, initially at least. Later, once one comes to know the person better, one hopes for the emergence of those traits of character that do deserve admiration. What the looks of another person offer is akin to what one seeks from a gorgeous sunset, a fine aroma, or a beautiful flower: something aesthetically pleasing. And why should that be a liability? Why are we somehow worse for desiring attractive natural features in our companions or dates, not to mention mates?

Certainly one can place too much emphasis on aesthetics. Yet, consider that for centuries the bulk of humanity couldn't even begin to exploit the aesthetic aspects of life—women and men simply got by, struggled for bare survival, and could neither ask for nor offer delightful pleasantries to each other. In our day, when finally millions of us are able to pay some attention to what may be aesthetically or otherwise pleasant about us—never mind that this begins with our natural attributes—why would some people denigrate those who accept such gifts? Why should those who can offer them be thought shallow?

The reason is actually political: no one is supposed to benefit while others are not doing so. Just as the well-to-do are denounced for having more than others—many blame them for enjoying life as long as there is one remaining poor person left in the universe—so with other benefits, especially ones people simply inherited through their genes.

Just think of how much hostility there is toward inherited wealth. Why? Because, for example, it is widely contended that we are all one, and if parts of us aren't getting enough, the rest of us should also suffer. Much political thinking goes along these lines. Humanity or the country or some other group is seen as a natural team to which all of us belong and the collective welfare of which is something we are all duty bound to support. If anyone is less well-off than others, that is considered intolerable.

Now if there is one thing that is prized nearly as highly as money, it is good looks or sex appeal. And it is often plausible to say that the owner of such an attribute has done little to achieve it. It is a native asset, more like inherited than created wealth.

Never mind that most attractive people must do something to keep fit and looking good. They are working with an advantage, and heaven deliver us from an advantage—it threatens the contemporary ideal of total uniformity among humankind.

Rather than embracing this awful egalitarianism, it makes much better sense to face the task of making the most of what we were born with and have been given by those around us who choose to give to us. If within these limits we do well, we probably are both fortunate and deserving; if we do badly, then we are the opposite. But in neither instance is playing Robin Hood with these benefits and liabilities justified. No one is justified in depriving us of what has been freely bestowed upon us.

And if a person is attractive, and gains by this good fortune, so be it. Those of us who have the chance to be with such people shouldn't have to give up this little delight in our lives simply to please those surly folks who cannot stand anyone being better off than others.

Why begrudge the rose its fate of not being an ugly weed? And why begrudge our luck in finding the rose?

Back to All
That's Beautiful*

Although it is something of a liability to declare oneself either an optimist or a pessimist—the suspicion arises that one may be working with preconceptions—I am indeed an optimist, but for solid reasons. I keep my eyes and ears open, and what I perceive daily confirms my optimism, despite some evidence to the contrary.

What all this comes from is the constant bellyaching I get from folks who have pronounced our age a moral and aesthetic, not to mention political, cesspool. You know, Robert Bork, with his depressing talk of *Slouching towards Gomorrah* (New York: Regan Books, 1996) and former *National Review* and now web columnist Joe Sobran and many others, with their dire judgments about modernity. Not only do these folks suffer from a case of self-induced pessimism, but their message seems to me to be thoroughly uninformed.

Over the years I have been a student of philosophy, reading some of the most exciting products of the human mind—as well as some of the most depressing stuff—to great profit. But apart from such works, I have also found reading fiction to be extremely rewarding. I caught on to this trick when I was only eight or nine, after picking up Hungarian translations of works by Mark Twain, Erle Stanley Gardner, Zane Grey, Max Brand, Karl May, and half a dozen others whose books I used to read into the wee hours of the night, under my blankets with a flashlight, to escape my mother's wrath for not getting enough sleep. This early proclivity for searching out the ways creative thinkers fashion alternate realities and personalities stuck with me, and to this day no matter how busy I am, no matter how full of tasks and challenges and complications my life is, I am always reading a novel by David Lodge, Winston Graham, W. Somerset Maugham, Thomas Mann, Graham Greene, Margaret Drabble, Barbara Pym, Mark Saltzman, or someone else — and there are many more I just cannot stop to list.

My mother used to drag me to classical concerts back in my early years, and while I mostly fell asleep — having spent the nights reading — this also showed me some astonishing examples of human creativity. Then came the theater, art museums and galleries, jazz and blues, and all the rest — including malls and amusement parks, deserts, the sea and the mountains, night clubs and promenades and friends, lovers, colleagues, and, especially, my kids — and slowly but surely I became convinced that life is rather good, all things fairly considered.

No, I didn't miss the horrors, either — I was born just six months before the outbreak of World War II and was right smack in the middle of it all, with bombs falling around me, sirens going off at all hours of the day, a city in near-total ruin, and lives destroyed or maimed, so how could I miss the evil that human beings were capable of? And then living under the brutal Communists and growing up with a similarly brutal Nazi-supporting father put me on notice about how rotten things and people can get. And I have had my share of pain and disease and calamity and guilt, too, so I'm not deluded about how bad things can be.

Yet, what I had to conclude, after some time, was that all in all life is good, and if one pays attention, one will not succumb to the temptation of dismissing it cavalierly as so many earnest and profound — or pretentious? — folks do. It is their insistence that there is something especially bad about the modern era, something soulless and dreadfully shallow, that keeps annoying me. All this dissing of bourgeois values by our literati Left and Right is just out to lunch, so far as I can judge.

I have tried to explain it in one way or another: maybe these folks just want to carp about something, wag their fingers, to create for themselves the illusion of being much more high and mighty than the rest of us; or perhaps they cannot differentiate between getting old, running down biologically, and being near death themselves, and the way the world is outside their heads; or maybe they just have indigestion too much and infuse their bad feelings into how the world looks to them. I am not sure, of course.

But I do know they are distorting how things really are — do they ever listen to music, look at paintings, attend plays, and, especially, read both nonfictional and fictional works? Don't they notice just how wonderful is the human ability to create, how it has filled the world with wonder and beauty, aside from some admittedly annoying trash?

I have not been alive in another age, so I do not have direct knowledge of how it all was in A.D. 300 or 400 B.C. or the 1400s, but I look into these periods regularly through the reports of those who lived then. And, all in all, I do not get the impression that those ages were so cool, comparatively speaking. Yes, the twentieth century had some of the worst manifestations of human evil and neglect, and much of this is going on right now, as well. But then not only nature but human choice manages to produce both good and bad in the world, and I do not believe that somehow in our time human evil has conquered. If you do, I recommend taking a closer look—read, listen, look, experience, and, most of all, do something interesting and valuable!

Entranced from the Start
by "Here's Johnny"

Orange County (California) Register, May 12, 1992

About ten years ago *TV Guide* ran an article on Johnny Carson in which the claim was made that the *Tonight Show*'s host appealed only to middle-class Americans. I wrote a letter, which was published, protesting this claim.

I, a Hungarian refugee raised in Europe until my late adolescence, have been a Carson fan from the start. I recall watching NBC-TV's tryouts to see who would take over after Jack Paar left, in the late summer of 1962. I was hospitalized at the time and stayed up for each of the performers, to see who would be most enjoyable to watch late at night, when the day ended and one didn't wish to retire with trouble on one's mind. Carson was clearly the hands-down winner.

As soon as I left Hungary, I knew I wanted to come to the United States, and I made the most of American entertainment in Europe—notably the Armed Forces Network radio station in Munich, Germany, where I lived for three years before coming to the United States. After I arrived, I found it helpful to take in some of the popular entertainment, partly because I was eager to adapt to American popular culture.

One favorite entertainer of mine was a disc jockey named Big Wilson on a Cleveland, Ohio, radio station. He spoke incredibly fast—I could only get about every fourth word he spoke—but I swore that in time I would fully understand him. That is one of the ways I learned English—I wanted to get the pronunciation down pat, not just the grammar and vocabulary. (In those days no one would have suggested that a refugee should be treated to bilingual education!)

I started to watch Jack Paar around 1958 and found the range of gossip on the show very interesting, though Paar's idiosyncrasies were often annoying. He really believed himself to be much more than an entertainer, or he feigned this belief, apparently thinking that there is something ignoble about just entertaining an audience.

When Carson took over, I realized how pleasant it can be to watch a very good and self-confident entertainer at work. Johnny never seemed to apologize for what his job amounted to, bringing some laughs and gossip into our lives, after we had coped with our daily routines and responsibilities. I admired that and still do.

But, of course, what was most appealing to me about Carson is probably what kept him on the air for all those years and why no one has ever come even close to unseating him: he is a master of comic timing. Even when his jokes fail to make it big, he is very quick at milking the failure for as much humor as he can extract from it. He never gives up. He is self-reflective in an unpretentious way that does not flaunt his skills and achievements but makes excellent use of them for the purpose for which he was hired, to keep us in stitches, or at least very pleasantly amused.

Carson's one fault is that he sometimes wants to match his guest's intellectual agility, which is clearly not always possible. He should not try to "out–Gore Vidal" Gore Vidal, "out–Bill Buckley" Bill Buckley. That is not his forte, and trying to go such folks one better makes him look insecure. That may be why in later years he stopped inviting such guests—he somehow didn't feel comfortable with them.

And his team should have realized this long ago; it didn't really add a lot to the *Tonight Show* with Johnny Carson to let Carl Sagan and his ilk show off their stuff. (Of course, some of this is a very close judgment call; Truman Capote, though something of an intellectual, had a number of entertaining quirks to his personality and so managed to be a good guest for Carson.)

But the real meat of the Johnny Carson program was (1) the monologue, (2) the guests, such as Buddy Hackett or Burt Reynolds, and (3) the hundreds of young, as well as established, comics whom Carson featured over the years.

A word about Ed McMahon. Some people find him irksome, what with his somewhat artificial guffaws, but he really did serve the show in just the capacity he was selected for early in Carson's career, as a sidekick. And the musical support of Doc Severinsen and his orchestra could not easily be matched either.

I, for one, want to thank Johnny Carson. I am glad he was paid well by NBC—he certainly added a small but very delightful dimension to the past thirty years of my life in these United States. Thanks, Mr. Carson. I will miss you.

Meanings of Christmas

Orange County (California) Register, December 24, 1984

I have this wish that we be spared this year all the talk about how Christmas is turning into a commercial orgy, how people shamelessly indulge their desires, whims, and materialistic concerns and thus forget the true spiritual meaning of the season.

When the world is clamoring for a better life, when we are wringing our hands about unemployment, hunger, destitution, and sickness, let us for once admit that what we really want is for everyone to produce a lot and buy a great deal. Why shouldn't Christmas be a time to want more and better and to resolve to do what is necessary to get it—earn more, work harder, produce, and create?

The spirituality of Christmas is mysterious, and it should be private and intimate. But the wish for nice gifts, the desire to please, the search for a good buy—these can be quite public. If there is more of it everywhere, the country, perhaps the world, can look forward to deflecting an economic depression.

Americans have for decades been the main hope of this world. That great revolutionary society, the Soviet Union, counts on America to feed its people, even as it condemns capitalism. The rest of the world sells us cars, oil, shoes, coffee, and more while we sell them some of what we make. We buy more than they do because we produce more and can afford more.

Except for a few, foreigners admire America, mainly because they know the value of freedom better than we do. That is why they wish to come here and why the dollar is so strong—they know which country is most likely to keep up its productivity, its economic prudence, which creates jobs and good investments.

We should keep it up. A Christmas brimming with goodies encourages people to do more for themselves. That is how progress can be maintained. We discover more, we learn more, we want more—and better—things, of course. A new piece of software, a new car, a new dress, a new book, even a new heart—and on and on. All of that is wonderful, even though it isn't all there is to life.

Wishing to be surrounded with interesting things, with sources of pleasure and satisfaction, is what everyone would like.

As an ex-European, I know that Americans work harder, more productively. They like the idea of fulfillment in life. They are practical, pragmatic, utilitarian; yet they are also generous, joyful, cheerful. Everywhere in America, one sees people walking about laughing, sitting around smiling, kidding, showing that above all they enjoy life, rather than regard it as a great pain.

So this Christmas, let us relax about our interest in all the goodies people want to sell us. We should enjoy shopping; we should defy the calls for feeling guilty and ashamed.

We should flaunt the fact that we like life here on Earth. We should indulge, sensibly, but unashamed. We should enjoy all there is to give, to take, to play with, to use, and think of what we might have next.

That is the way the world can be better fed and housed, become more healthy and even wiser, since the time required to gain wisdom is affordable only when one has some wealth.

Christmas could have far worse effects than making us run about chasing good times, good buys, good gifts, and good cheer. It could pit us against one another. It could make us feel resentful, envious, and jealous. Isn't it far better that it prompts us to cheer, to seek pleasure?

We should not be denied such innocent hedonism. We are creatures of this Earth, and our nature is creative, inventive, exploratory, adventurous.

Why be surprised, then, that we would seek and make newer and better things? That is most human of us, indeed.

Affirm the Joy of Living Right, Here on Earth

Yuma (Arizona) Sun, September 11, 2002

September 11, 2002, is near, and I wish to urge everyone to use this anniversary of the terrible massacre of innocent human beings, most of them conscientious business professionals, to affirm loudly and clearly the value of living here on Earth as happily, decently, and prosperously as possible.

That is what those who perished in the World Trade Center were striving to do, for themselves and their loved ones. I believe we should make no apologies for this and indeed celebrate it joyfully, in the spirit of "in your face," if we must, to all those who resent us for it, who want to intimidate us all, who try to make us feel ashamed for our "materialistic" tendencies.

Materialistic my foot! Living a natural human life is no more materialistic than painting a beautiful painting is just because it is done on a canvas, using paints, brushes, and other worldly objects in the process. Human life here on Earth is, of course, directly dependent on the stuff that surrounds us and, yes, is us. We are part of nature, and this is no liability but something to make the most of.

Nature itself is a very diverse system, from the most simple to the unbelievably complex aspects of it, ourselves. Here we are, beings with the ability to think, write, sing, paint, make deals, construct the most exquisite artifacts, and so on—as well as do a lot that isn't so commendable. That is just how we are, and to be successful as this kind of being involves, to a substantial extent, prospering as much as we can.

There are those, of course, who begrudge us all this big time. Just recently, in Johannesburg, South Africa, a meeting took place where a lot of people were bellyaching about how the developed countries of the world are not doing enough to help those in the undeveloped parts. (One may wonder how much of the Earth's resources, the wasting of which is allegedly of such great concern, were spent on this shindig anyway?)

What exactly do the billions who are poor throughout the globe want? They want what those in the developed parts have. Yet, how is this goal to be achieved? Freedom is the answer, not more regimentation by a bunch of politicians who are mostly good at empty rhetoric.

But why should politicians say anything of substance when that would alert us to the fact that they have little, if anything, to offer that will actually help anyone? Politicians mostly urge us to agree to their robbing Peter to pay Paul. They do not do anything constructive themselves, not like people in business, engineering, education, or the arts. They facilitate looting, and that is what they propose, no matter what the crisis that affords them the excuse for it.

No, I do not think that politicians are all crooks, but most of them have no idea of what their real job is, helping to secure our basic, natural human rights. That is the oath the politician takes, in principle, not to solve all our problems for us; at least the politician does who acknowledges that citizens are adults, not invalids or dependent children.

Sadly, even when our politicians claim they are protecting us from terrorists and others who threaten to violate our rights, these politicians, too, are violating our rights under the pretext that this is needed now. Yet, way before modern terrorism was invented, politicians everywhere used such pretexts at every turn, whether to fight disease, bad weather, or poverty. They are like those members of the police who use excessive force when they say they are fighting crime, thereby making crime fighting just another instance of crime commission.

In any case, let us not be discouraged by how ineptly politicians and even the police defend us. Let us not be persuaded that there is something wrong with our efforts to live well and prosper here on Earth. That, I believe, is one of the best means by which we can answer our irrational critics who would have us return to the Stone Age and suffer in the name of one or another false idol, rather than do our best to live right as human beings who belong here on Earth and need to succeed in the midst of nature.

Afterword: Last Reflections

What I Have Done and Why

So much of what erudite people tell us deals with our motives. Why did Enron executives mess up what seemed like a savvy big business? Why did bin Laden direct terrorists to the World Trade Center and the Pentagon? Why did Lincoln suspend the principles of habeas corpus?

Reference to some motive or drive that leads people to do what they do is then made as an answer to these questions. As if it were so easy.

In fact, though, we do things for many reasons; our motives are rarely just this or that but usually a collage. And if a piece of that collage were missing, we could have done something entirely different.

For me, the explanation of how I've led my life probably lies in a broad range of facts, some having to do with my personality or temperament, some with my circumstances, some with my understanding of what matters most, some with what I've learned from others, and most of it with some combination of all these and others. Having been born in a country under the heavy influence of the Nazis, which then got taken over by Communists, and then managing to escape only to land in the home of a father with unambiguous anti-Semitic and fascist convictions—all the while being a ferocious reader of novels from Hungary, Germany, and America—I suppose all these factors in my past made a difference. Yet, I am also convinced that I brought to the table a particular, idiosyncratic way of making these factors matter in my life.

Once my late friend and mentor Ernest van den Haag, who among other things was a psychoanalyst, told me that I could probably murder someone and get off by pleading insanity, given my history, especially with my rather brutal upbringing. My mother, though often sweet, was a fanatical athlete whose method of discipline consisted mainly of slapping me around and using a horsewhip to beat on my thighs so when I'd go to school wearing shorts, I'd be picked on and laughed at. My father, in whose care fortunately I spent only a few years, was far worse. Nightly beatings left me utterly bewildered; I was baffled as to what was going on, why this torrent of anger and violence was in my life.

No, I wasn't some angel kid, of course. I had some of the discipline coming but rarely with the ferocity and anger my mother and later my father showed toward me. (Yet, consider their circumstances — it strikes me that they, especially my mother, had some excuses for their misconduct.) Still, none of that stopped me from living a kid's life, as well. My fondness for girls started early, my unceasing reading of fiction nearly at the same time, and I also did all the playful things to be expected from a child anywhere. When I came to America, I found myself confused, alone, and in need of some orientation, which is why, shortly after I ran away from home on my eighteenth birthday, it seemed not only prudent but wise to join the U.S. Air Force, where I got to think things through in relative leisure. In particular, I started to read philosophy while riding the base bus to and from work, even while standing at my post as an air policeman. I also discovered Ayn Rand and the wonders of travel — indirectly, through what I learned from some officer friends in the little theater group I helped found — and why it probably would be better to go to college than to take a job with the Pennsylvania highway patrol, a plan of action I at first conceived for myself.

Once I discovered that learning was exciting and rewarding, I also found my past to be a source of interest. I found out that an important question for everyone concerns what kind of community they should foster around themselves. Having experienced communism and elements of fascism, and having known implicitly and tacitly at first, and by direct experience later, that the promise of freedom is much better than these, I wanted to explore whether I was right about this or was just telling myself a story to rationalize having left Hungary. So, of all the subjects I explored in my earlier night school and later full-time college courses, philosophy popped up as the right one for me to tackle. I just really wanted to know what's right and why. There seemed to be no subject other than philosophy that promised to shed light on that matter in comparable depth.

But then I also had a yen for expressing my own hunches, convictions, questions, worries, and judgments, those I garnered from my philosophical and related readings and conversations with friends. And some were even original, though I cannot recall now which. So, very early on, even before going to college, I began writing letters to the editor, partly as a way to put into practice my hard-earned yet wobbly knowledge of English, partly to try to influence people, especially in places of power, to consider certain ideas more seriously than they seemed to want to.

From letter writing I went on to short essays, mostly for my school paper and then for the *Freeman* (now called *Ideas on Liberty*), ending up by helping to found a more serious version of an already budding magazine, *Reason*. Indeed, back in graduate school I had already been criticized by some of my professors—as I mentioned in the preface to this book—for being a bit quick with voicing my views; why didn't I act more humbly, more tentatively, as a good analytic philosopher should? (That was a joke—most analytic philosophers I knew were nothing if not smug and arrogant!) And when I challenged a local TV station about broadcasting ads for savings bonds, in order to show the injustice of banning cigarette ads because they were controversial, I was dismissed as just having some kind of compulsion to say something on a host of topics. Well, but was it a compulsion or rather a realization that there should be more good sense going around about public affairs? I thought the latter—I never felt as if I couldn't put aside my pen because I just had to write, no. I wanted to write—but I also wanted to do a lot else and did, partly to learn how to write and talk well enough to earn an audience. And this took time.

Of course many times I was told I might be too taken with my own ideas—why didn't I just listen more? Well, I did and do a lot of listening—reading, taking part in discussions, reflecting, revising, and so forth. But who of those who give expression to their ideas, questions, puzzles, criticisms, and wonder prizes humility above all? I gather all who chime in, whatever the content of their thought, take it that doing so matters and is needed for reaching decisions about how we should live, how our communities should be shaped. The issue isn't, I thought, remaining silent or speaking up but whether one speaks up thoughtfully, carefully, with good purpose.

My faults are probably many, but perhaps—contrary to some suggestions—they do not include my being a bit too prolific, considering what I choose to write on, mainly the vitality of human freedom and its proper institutional protection. This choice comes not from false pride but from a sense of what I can only consider valid urgency. Even in the midst of crisis, as I am doing the needed damage control— for instance, dealing with one of my children's reckless experiments with drugs or doomed romance, an auto accident, or a financial meltdown—I try to keep half an eye, at least, on the fate of liberty and on whatever threatens to take it from us. The same with times when I might lie back to enjoy a moment of triumph, the euphoria of doing well at something—I find the point about the price of liberty being eternal vigilance nearly impossible to lay aside.

For better or worse, I am convinced that too little of the kind of thinking I have come to see as sensible manages to get on the agenda of prominent forums, so I try very hard to get it there, period. And I'll continue to do this, even if the volume may strike some as too great. That's because if my part in the continuing conversation about the best way for people to live together helps even a little to make the world a more thoughtful and better place—helps encourage us to be more fully human and civilized—then maybe it is not too presumptuous to think that my contribution has been of value—both to me and to those I love. Which is gratifying and certainly helps make this part-time pundit's life worth living!

Try it yourself and see!

Index